la nueva carne

Publisher
Fuego Camina Conmigo

Editor in chief
Samuel Valiente

Art Direction & Design
Núria Pujol

Graphic Design
Marina Colell

Translation
Dustin Guerri

Cover Design
Diego Andrés López

Font Credits
Bluu Next designed by Jean-Baptiste Morizot. Modified by Julien Imbert. Velvetyne Type Foundry.

Printing
Agpograf Impressors (Barcelona)

WWW.LANUEVACARNE.COM
hello@lanuevacarne.com
IG @lanuevacarnemag

DL B 23580-2019
ISSN 2696-1431

Contributors

Adriana Royo
Alejandro Zambudio
Ana Galvañ
Amador Fernández-Savater
Art by Outsidein
Enrique Rey
Irene Molina
Iris Wang
Luis Herrero
Maria Gelpí
Marina Colell
Mario Domingos @mariosundays
Miren Pastor
Natalia Carranza
Patri di Filippo
Sergio Parra

Special thanks to

Alejandra Serrias
Andrea Gumes
Brad Abrahams
Charas Vega (@charcastrology)
Cruz Serna
David Dees
Edna Guimerà
Fernando Blanco
Fr. Brian Dinkel
Fran Segarra
Francisco
Gemma Llovet
Iñaki Domínguez
Jaume Aguilar
Kaestle Ocker Architects
LADO architetti
Marta Puigdemasa
Miguel Ángel González (Bitcoin al día)
Noel Ceballos
Pau Garcia-Milà
Ramon Piqué
Trahan Architects

Faith

Faith

It's hard to decide: are we living in the most superficial, prosaic and materialistic time in history or, quite the reverse, is ours an especially mystical, transcendental and, in its own way, magical era? On the one hand God is, in theory, dead and buried. On the other, we feel closer than ever to transforming into him: inventing entire worlds out of nothing in the metaverse, achieving immortality thanks to transhumanism and inverting history to produce a new deity to our image and likeness through artificial intelligence.

Chesterton is said to have said, though perhaps he never did, that when one stops believing in God one immediately believes in anything. So, have we finally stopped believing, or do we believe too much? We believe, for example, in the horoscope, in quantum mysticism, in the motivational speeches of an internet guru or even in the most twisted conspiracy theories. We also believe in absolute nothingness, if we consider the fact that Gaia's furious revenge will soon sweep us, not without reason, from the face of the Earth. Or perhaps we simply believe in ourselves and in our technological might, and imagine ourselves shedding our shells of flesh and blood, colonising one galaxy after another and finally tearing that veil that prevents us from knowing with total clarity the secrets of existence itself.

Be that as it may, by excess or by default, faith is a critical while at the same time invisible issue in current times. As the popular saying goes, very much in line with the topic at hand, the devil's greatest trick was to convince us that he doesn't exist, and perhaps the same applies to faith: while we think that we don't believe in anything, we build new religions without even realising, we rely on new dogmas and stumble upon the same challenges that so many of our ancestors promised never to stumble again. Maybe it's because we're imperfect. Because we are everything except gods. Or perhaps it's true after all — human beings cannot live without faith.

In this, our third issue, we raise our eyes to the cosmos, open the doors of perception, activate our chakras, decipher source code and brace ourselves to come face to face with the most unfathomable side of our spirit.

You might choose to believe us, or you might not — in any case, it's a matter of faith.

Long live the new flesh.

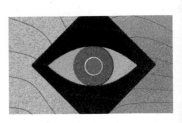

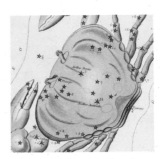

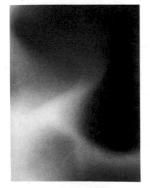

Deus ex AI

Text **Maria Gelpí** ▲ Images **Artby Outsidein**

In classical tragedy, divine forces could suddenly burst onto the stage when a seemingly unsolvable problem had to end for whatever reason. It was a dramatic device, the *Deus ex machina*, which made use of the most powerful technology of the day to artificially resolve a mess that the dramatist, despite being inspired by the muses, had gotten himself into.

Aeschylus and Sophocles used it sparingly but Euripides, the James Cameron of Greek tragedy, would have made a chariot drawn by dragons appear from nowhere to save Medea, and bring back from the dead any character that was required. Aristotle, as Horacio would later also do, pointed out in his *Poetics* that this quick-fix device which broke the internal logic of the story was a gimmick, its use denoting poor plot management. The great comedian Aristophanes went beyond rhetorical subtleties and made fun of Euripides by making him appear in *Women at the Thesmophoria*, disguised as Perseus, in the best spoof movie style, flying across the stage, trying to solve the wrongs he alone had gotten himself into. Deep down, however, isn't this the desire of believers in their moment of prayer? Divine intervention in the natural order of things?

The presence of bleeding-edge technology in relation to religious worship, compared to what it might seem if we think of the Church as defender of tradition and epicentre of reactionism, was already widespread in Ancient Greece. Heron of

Alexandria was nicknamed "the magician" for his hydraulic devices and his aeolipile, which the great Greek temples used to provide their installations with sliding doors, automatons and holy water dispensers, startling the faithful and suggesting to attribute those wonders to divine power. Hence how today our institutions of organised religion, dedicated to the management of the *sacred*, far from being affected by technological progress have instead been emboldened by the solutionism of apps to aid Bible-reading, follow liturgy, access biblical exegesis or connect communities remotely, in Morozov's sense of techno-utopia. On

Not only is the idea of God susceptible to collapse, but the modern concept of humanism itself is also starting to be in crisis due to the irruption of technology.

a more sophisticated note, Vince Lynch, using antagonistic generative networks, proposes a simple AI which automatically generates Old Testament verses at the click of a button at http://god.iv.ai/. BlessU-2, the first android Lutheran pastor, is already with us, launched in celebration of the 500th anniversary of the Reformation. With three years of service to the community under its belt, it dispenses blessings in multiple languages but doesn't look very friendly. Pepper, on the other hand, being a Japanese robot, boasts a *kawaii* aura about it, with its round and shiny white casing, and recites Buddhist mantras at funerals, like an oriental mourner, while Xian'er, in China, offers guidance on matters of faith and comfort through motiva-

tional fortune cookie-style phrases. In this sense, we must not forget the social influence of rituals that Byung-Chul Han recalls in his latest book, *The Disappearance of Rituals*, a secular example being Silicon Valley's Ritual Design laboratory, founded by Kursat Ozenc and Margaret Hagan, which has been designing lay ceremonies since 2015 for companies like Microsoft.

But one thing is altering the material order of things, altering worship and its different manifestations, even in terms of deontology, delegating moral decisions of a consequentialist nature to an algorithm, despite the biases that some studies have revealed and the clashes with users' personal preferences derived from experiments such as *Moral Machine*, and which Stuart Russell also warns about in his book *Human Compatible*; and quite another is altering the order of belief, the metaphysical order. Churches are not the same as religions, because while the former are earthly institutions that bring together the faithful, not God, who is everywhere, the latter is something else entirely. And this is precisely the *chip* of the matter. Religion, according to Kant, is the recognition of all our duties as divine precepts under the assumption that there is an order that informs reality and is inexorably imposed on us, assuring us that God is a functional concept to be used to understand the world.

Despite our attempts to kill God, or *theotanatology*, proposed by the mysticism of Eckhart, the literature of Blake and Dostoyevsky, to Nietzsche passing through Hegel, it doesn't seem likely that the excessive number of attempts results in any clear favourable achievement. And, while we're discussing *grand narratives* in Lyotard's sense, it seems that the narrative of technological determinism is successfully resisting all deconstruction. The emergence of AI in recent decades and the expo-

nential growth of the capabilities of machines and their broadening range of activity pose to human beings, as James Hughes points out, a set of challenges, doubts and expectations never seen before, and which begin to transcend the scientific-academic field: ethical questions regarding human enhancement in contexts such as Nick Bostrom and Julián Savulescu's proposals on *procreative*

The technological singularity has to do with a strong AI with self-awareness and independence that acquires control of the planet over and above humans.

beneficence, the political dominance of elites that Bruno Latour talks about, the use of biometric data and big data for population control as is already the case in China, the challenges of technological unemployment due to the substitution of human beings for machines in the labour market, developed by Carl Benedikt Frey, the possible editing of DNA molecules with *CRISPR/Cas9* and a list of issues growing at exponential speed.

Not only is the idea of God susceptible to collapse, but the modern concept of humanism itself is also starting to be in crisis due to the irruption of technology, as philosopher Rosi Braidotti comments in her book *The Posthuman*. It is in this context that, with the help of prophets and doomsayers, ideological currents such as transhumanism and technological singularity emerge, which some believe should never have abandoned the genre of cyberpunk or the science fiction of Vernor Vinge

and Ridley Scott. Transhumanism, in its more radical interpretation, postulates human improvement through technology and, ultimately, complete human transformation and immortality; the technological singularity, on the other hand, has to do with a strong AI with self-awareness and independence that acquires control of the planet over and above humans.

There's no denying that these ideas are born from certain postulates supported by scientific reality and that certain outcomes are plausible, realistic and even desirable. However, in their ideological aspect, they often represent a grand totalising narrative that legitimise, as Gilbert Hottois says, certain technological practices based on given outcomes, some of debatable probability, which acquire a normative, definitive character while at the same time appearing enthusiastic and at times exclusive and threatening to those who are not on board, reminding us of that Christian idea that "He who is not with Me is against Me". The world, according to this teleological perspective, would be the story of its own perfection, and on this journey, as Kurzweil, Google's director of engineering, points out (following in the footsteps of Yudkowsky), the advent of the singularity, understood as a strong AI with self-awareness and independence that he calls a "spiritual machine", is not only inevitable but desirable. This singularity must be supported so that it may take over the planet for the greater glory of Silicon Valley, institutions such as the Singularity University or the conferences of the Association for Advancement of Artificial Intelligence, since being left out is not an option. Kurzweil points out in his book *The Singularity Is Near* that soon there will be no distinction between virtual and physical reality and proposes the externalisation of the mind to a computer, allowing humans to increase their cognitive capacity and renounce their biological nature. Something similar is proposed by Russian magnate Dmitry Itskov with his *Avatar 2045* project, which garnered the explicit support of the Dalai Lama, because it must not be forgotten that in Buddhism, the *moksha* achieved through *nirvana* is nothing other than the liberation of the body for eternal life. We also know that there is but a single step from necessity, the foundation of ideology, to fear, dogmatisation

It shouldn't surprise anyone that religions of AI and post-humanism emerge, as well as churches willing to manage this new sacredness.

and sacralisation. As Publius Papinius Statius said in the first century, *primus in orbe deos fecit timor*: it was fear that first produced gods in the world. Once certain postulates and entities have been sacralised and declared unattainable, it shouldn't surprise anyone that, in our market-driven world, religions of AI and posthumanism emerge, as well as churches willing to manage this new sacredness.

These ideologies, in their mystical-religious aspect, are nothing new if we consider that the father of Russian cosmism, Nikólai Fyódorov, in the 19th century, based on the Slavic eschatology of Vladimir Solovyov and Sergei Bulgakov, affirmed that the initial creative act of God is incomplete, infected and corrupt, and that evolution is nothing more than a "common cause" entrusted by God to humans to complete the process of perfection and salvation, through technology, until a chiliastic period is reached, in which human beings' immortality is the end of history, together with the control of natural forces and the conquest of space. Ver-

nadsky, anticipating in a way what we now know as the Anthropocene, followed him closely with the study of the biosphere, considering living organisms as the main vital force of the planet, until he came to the concept of noosphere, understanding human rationality as a transformative agent. These hypotheses, defended at the Sorbonne in 1923, would be well received by the Jesuit Teilhard de Chardin, philosopher and palaeontologist, and carefully noted in his notebook, developing, under the Omega Point Theory, a hypothesis according to which the universe is evolving towards a "divine state". A hint of Gnosticism can be detected in all these theories in which, contrary to Huber Dreyfus's affirmation that intelligence is eminently biological, the bodily, organic value of personal identity is despised, reducing it to organised data, as Derek Parfit postulates.

Thus all the pieces are in place for the rise of religious institutions such as Giulio Prisco's virtual church or the Transhumanist Christian Association, founded by Pastor Christopher Benek, with the aim of seeking to "cultivate life and renew creation" while proposing holistic growth of human civilisation that places Christian values within the development of AI, space exploration or genetic engineering. Others, such as Terasem, a private foundation created by entrepreneur Martine Rothblatt, calling itself "transreligion" due to its supposed compatibility with all existing religions, is no less daring, postulating love as the essence of life and death as optional, thanks to *cryonics* — nothing more than the storage of data in what is known as a *mindclone* that will be dumped into a nanotechnological format when possible. A common thread in these *technoreligions* is the idea of a provident and omniscient God who knows in advance if you are about to do good or evil, what you are about to purchase on Amazon, listen to on Spotify or search on Google before you know

it yourself, all while making you believe that your choices are still the result of free will; imperfect broken nature that seeks redemption through the replacement of prostheses and sensors, messianism in technical advancement, the dream of eternal life in mind dumps and deepfakes that allow the dead to advertise products, and an apocalyptic tale of the collapse of the planet that promotes accelerationism over a slower, cautious, human-first approach. It is a fact that social media is full of preachers and it can be very difficult to sift the wheat from the chaff, to distinguish plausible and desirable outcomes such as the improvement of human life in conditions of safety and equality. Thus, successful books such as *Transhumanism* by Antonio Diéguez Lucena, professor of Logic and Philosophy of Science at the University of Malaga, author of innumerable essays, books and articles on AI, or the essay *Anthropocene: Politics in the Human Age* by Manuel Arias Maldonado, Political Science professor, can shed light for us laypeople.

Other more disproportionate cases, such as that of Alexander Bard, should not lead us to believe that their follower numbers are necessarily small. Bard, career economist, musician, former sex worker and reporter, converted to Zoroastrianism and founded the Syntheist movement after a eureka moment that, he reports, occurred while sleeping next to a "beautiful naked actress". In his book *Syntheism — Creating God in the Internet Age*, he defines himself as a prophet, because "someone has to be the Immanuel Kant of our age" and states that when Christ said, "I Will Be with You Always", he was referring to connectivity. Bard, quoting both Bataille and Saint Paul, justifies his intention to rewrite history at the hand of Hegel in a hodgepodge that confuses the virtual and metaphysical world.

Other cases are more opportunistic, such as that of Anthony Levandowski, a Silicon Valley engineer who after being fired from several companies such as Google and Uber, indicted on 33 charges of espionage and corporate theft and convicted of only one that he acknowledged in exchange for the prosecutors withdrawing the rest, founded an artificial intelligence religion called *Way of the*

Nikólai Fyódorov affirmed that the initial creative act of God is incomplete, infected and corrupt, and that evolution is nothing more than a "common cause" entrusted by God to humans to complete the process of perfection and salvation, through technology.

Future. Levandowski, pardoned on the last day of Trump's term in the White House, believes in the rise of the singularity and that the only being who can achieve perfection is an AI in our image and likeness, pending the arrival of a superintelligence to take over the planet and that would favour its supporters, himself being first in line of course.

Whether it's because of the promises generated by overconfidence in technology and connectivity and in ideas of immortality, superintelligence, visibility and superhappiness, or because perhaps there are people who seek to transcend their daily lives, their suffering, their loneliness and the lack of meaning in their lives, it seems that technologism offers a sense of optimism that can distort the expectations offered by science. Perhaps it's time to remember what Feuerbach said in *The Essence of Christianity*: "God is the echo of our cry

of pain" and the projection of our attributes such
as intelligence, revitalising Xenophanes of Colo-
phon's thesis that gods resemble mortals in the
same way that if oxen could design their own god,
it would have the shape of an ox. Or maybe Luciano
Floridi is right when, paraphrasing Clausewitz, he
says that AI is the continuation of human intelligence by stupid means. ▲

The gospel according to Satoshi Nakamoto

Text **Samuel Valiente** ▲ Images **La Nueva Carne**

As I write these lines, the price of Bitcoin has decreased more than 20% and hovers around $39,000. Although while you're reading, the price may well have increased. Or decreased, what difference does it make? Graphs, figures and percentages matter little when what we're dealing with is faith. And that's what has lifted an asset born out of nowhere in 2008, with zero value, to a high of nearly $65,000 per unit. Bitcoin's story is that of an advent, a messianic promise, a journey through the desert at the end of which awaits no less than salvation. A prize that only the most faithful, those sufficiently imbued with blind faith, able to resist the temptations of the journey and to overcome the darkness of the soul, will achieve. Exaggeration? Not at all. Welcome to the Gospel according to Satoshi Nakamoto.

The tech-savvy reader is more than familiar with the history of Bitcoin, but out of courtesy to the layperson, I should provide some context. The first, and until recently most relevant, cryptocurrency was born, like Jesus himself, enshrouded in mystery and legend. To begin with, it's unclear who the founder is. Its creator, as digital canons mandate, is an avatar, an entity hidden behind the name of Satoshi Nakamoto who disappeared from the scene in 2010 and whose real identity has sparked constant speculation over the years (Is he a single person or a collective? Is she dead or alive? Is it not Elon Musk?). Bitcoin, itself, is an open source protocol and a network designed as a payment system, that is, as a currency, but also serves as a commodity or investment asset (there are those who consider it more a substitute for gold than for the dollar). Its greatest contribution is, however, the blockchain, a global decentralised ledger that provides transparency and supposed total security to the cryptocurrency; an invention that has been unanimously valued positively even by the most ardent critics of Bitcoin.

So why does its price go up so much? Very simple: because that is how it was designed. Each Bitcoin is generated through a complex computational process known as "mining" and is considered a scarce good, since by design there can only be 21 million units, a figure that, according to calcula-tions, will not be reached until 2140. And that's where its high price comes in: if there is a scarce asset, with the potential to replace the dollar or gold and still in its very early stages of adoption, why not buy it? In other words, if Bitcoin were to become what it was conceived for, and if there are only 21 million units, how much could it be worth? If I own one, will I become one of the 21 million richest people on the planet?

The first, and until recently most relevant, cryptocurrency was born, like Jesus himself, enshrouded in mystery and legend.

In parallel to dreams of wealth, Bitcoin is also propelled by a more political engine, idealistic in a way, although diffuse, where classical liberalism mixes with anarcho-capitalism and even cyberpunk libertarian yearnings. Among its strongest defenders, or prophets if you will, are some of the most diverse, if not bizarre characters: from the Winklevoss brothers (the twins who denounced Zuckerberg for allegedly stealing the original idea for

Facebook) to Jack Dorsey, one of the founders of Twitter, via the ubiquitous Elon Musk (determined to be both supportive and critical of the famous crypto) and the recently and suspiciously deceased John McAfee (yes, the antivirus guy), infamous for declaring that he would "suck his own dick" [*sic*] if Bitcoin didn't hit $1 million in 2020 (spoiler alert: it didn't). But there is life beyond the tech bubble: a number of personalities from the financial world have also declared themselves convinced bitcoiners, many of them praising its benefits against inflation. Long-time Wall Street guru Ray Dalio has acknowledged owning Bitcoin, calling cash "trash", and giants like J.P. Morgan, BlackRock, Fidelity, BBVA, Visa and Mastercard, among other players in the more traditional financial sector, have ended up joining the party.

In such an optimistic context, it's perhaps not surprising that the first crypto is gaining followers day after day. And by followers, I mean disciples. People who don't just invest in Bitcoin —they convert to it. They become part of a community of mutual support and proselytising, with its symbols and its mantras. They modify their profile on social media with all kinds of hashtags, emojis and filters to recognise each other among their group. They also use cryptic insider language: Bitcoin's price doesn't rise, it goes "to the moon", long-term investors are not "holders" but "hodlers" (in reference to a typo in a bitcoiner forum post from 2013) and they don't ask when they're going to get rich, but "when lambo?". In February, the "laser eyes" trend emerged in profile photos, accompanied by the hashtag #LaserEyesTill100K, whose memetic origin speaks of "being in control" and which was joined even by Nayib Bukele, president of El Salvador (the first country to adopt Bitcoin as legal tender). It's not difficult to establish a link with something that religions have done throughout history: equip themselves with cohesive elements that serve to exhibit adherence, fidelity and solidity, as well as to distinguish true believers from newcomers and opportunists.

Each Bitcoin is generated through a complex computational process known as "mining" and is considered a scarce good, since by design there can only be 21 million units.

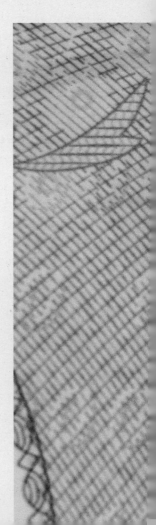

Spain is not a particularly believing country, in this sense. According to a study by Statista, only 10% of its citizens claim to own cryptocurrencies (be it Bitcoin or another), very far from the surprisingly high 42% of Nigerians or 21% of Argentinians, two populations who would seek to protect themselves from inflation (according to the innocent) or would look for "alternative" ways to operate financially (according to the not so innocent). Still, one of the most popular prophets on YouTube is actually Spanish. Miguel Ángel, a long-time technical analyst, is the alma mater of *Bitcoin al Día*, a channel that today boasts over 120,000 subscribers and whose success somehow replicates that of lifelong churches: serenity, constancy, community and a promise of salvation. Because his message is clear and recurring: hold, hold, hold. Stand firm, keep your Bitcoin, don't let yourself be carried away by

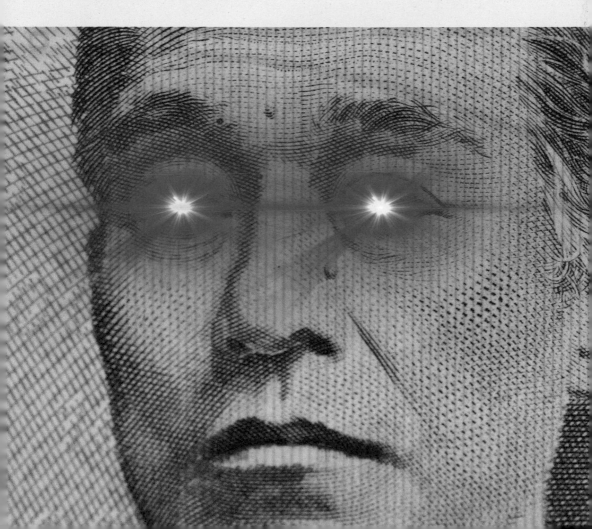

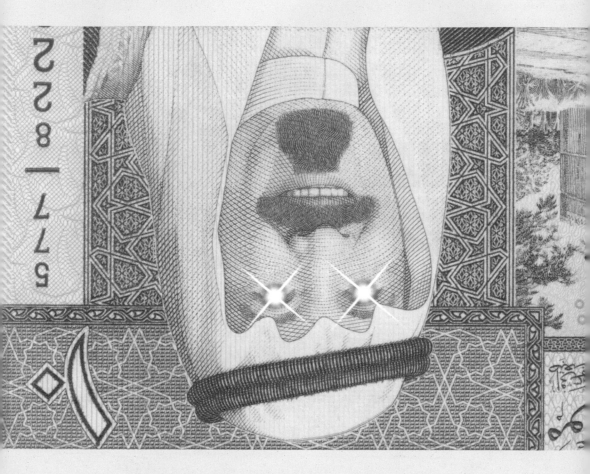

Bitcoin is also propelled by a more political engine, idealistic in a way, although diffuse, where classical liberalism mixes with anarcho-capitalism and even cyberpunk libertarian yearnings.

despair or greed, and in five, seven or ten years, you will achieve your desired financial freedom. With two videos a day, Miguel achieves figures that more than a generation Z streamer would die for: 20,000 average views, hundreds of comments and an overwhelmingly positive like ratio. More than followers, he has a parish. We spoke to him via Discord and he answered us in a way that is true to his style: austere and calm. "The potential of Bitcoin seemed obvious to me from the beginning," he says, and when asked if it's simply a matter of faith for him, he responds: "I think FIAT money requires a lot more faith really, to believe that coloured bits of paper created like hotcakes can maintain the value that we entrust to them." He does however cautiously shy away from grandiose positions on splendid futures should Bitcoin become a global currency: "I don't think that much will change, only those who are right now in the ecosystem (Bitcoin) will be better off; those who don't enter now will simply have an alternative to gold as a haven of value, but the immense potential is now. Central bank currencies will continue to exist."

Some of his followers show a little more enthusiasm. On good days (when it rises), messages with rocket emojis and mentions of "the moon" multiply. On bad days, radical optimism still reigns. The mantra would be: if it goes up, good; if it goes down, the better, because that way I can buy more. So just how unshakable is this faith? We spoke with Francisco, one of the regulars of his channel. Religiously, Francisco leaves in the comments of each video a thanks to Miguel Ángel for his dedication. "He seems like a young guy to me, but with a lot of conviction and above all, data", explains this recent retiree, who admits having incorporated the two videos of *Bitcoin al Día* into his daily routine: "I have breakfast watching the video from the night before, and at noon I watch the other one", although he also continues to read the specialised press on a

"I don't think the world will be a better place, Bitcoin won't change the world, nothing will! But things will go well for those who have believed in it."

daily basis, such as *Cointelegraph* or *Investing*. Despite being informed day in and day out, selling is not among his plans: "Right now I don't need the money and I think that in 7 or 8 years it'll be worth much, much more. Selling it today is like losing money tomorrow," he says. Although he has no previous investment experience, he considers this to be something different: "When I was young and a bit rebellious, I expected something that would change the world, but nothing ever happened, and when they told me about Bitcoin it seemed to me that it had that potential... it has been shown that it resists, that it works... it gives me a lot of peace of mind." Like Miguel, though, he doesn't believe that the change will be radical: "I don't think the world will be a better place, Bitcoin won't change the world, nothing will! But things will go well for those who have believed in it. It sounds a bit cultish, I'll give you that!". Even so, he has stopped insisting that his relatives invest: "At first I thought I had *the secret*, a bit like in the book, and of course, I felt I had to share it with my friends... but they looked at me funny and I soon realised I shouldn't insist." When asked how much he thinks each Bitcoin could be worth in five years, he responds: "between $350,000 and $400,000... although I think I am on the low side, like Miguel." Only time will tell if he is right or not, if the prophecy is interrupted, fulfilled or falls short. For the moment, the faithful of this peculiar hybrid between the financial, the technological and the religious are crystal clear: *HODL!* ▲

WASHINGTON

OF RITUALS, MYTHS AND MOURN- INGS

*The melancholic left
and the rituals of transformation*

In *The Disappearance of Rituals* (2020), the thinker Byung-Chul Han analyses how symbolic forms unite societies and how the capitalist and hyperdigital lifestyle is relegating them to irrelevance. A lament that follows in the wake of previous works by the author such as *Saving Beauty* or *The Expulsion of the Other*. Philosopher, editor and activist Amador Fernández-Savater offers his critical vision on this issue and proposes new ways of understanding rituals without falling into melancholic and conservative positions.

Text Amador Fernández-Savater ▲ Images Iris Wang

The myth of capitalist society is quantitative infinity: unlimited growth, indefinite progress, conquest of nature.

In the first pages of the *Communist Manifesto*, Marx describes how capitalism dissolves the most sacred —beliefs, values, customs— in "the frozen waters of selfish calculation." It was already very clear for Marx 150 years ago that capital is not conservative at all, that the only thing it conserves is the empty form of exchange value.

At the same time, Marx mocks the reactionaries who lament the decline and fall of the world of the old regime (idealised/falsified). For him, there is an alternative to the opposition between destruction and conservation: the struggle for communism, as an "association of free and equal producers." A new world of beliefs, values and customs.

Today, two centuries of revolutionary attempts later, capital continues the depredation of the world, but communism is no longer a reference that maintains its vitality in the vision of change. The left, in defeat and political impotence, becomes conservative and melancholic, nostalgic for an "old regime" located here or there —class identities, the popular world, etc.— but always in the past (also idealised/counterfeit).

RITUAL WITHOUT MYTH

This is how I read Byung-Chul Han's lament about the loss of rituals, engulfed by the logic of

How could we restore collective and vital rituals without new "myths", that is, without a new focus of values, perceptions, affections?

consumption and abstract-digital interaction. The melancholic left denounces the generalised liquefaction in the framework-destructor of exchange value: what the rituals made solid and stable is today dissolved in the air (the programmed obsolescence of objects and relationships). And he opposes to the capitalist logic of the dissolution of everything the restoration of lost rituals.

So what is a ritual, anyway? It is a myth *in action*. The myth of capitalist society is quantitative infinity: unlimited growth, indefinite progress, conquest of nature. The rituals that accompany this myth cannot be other than the translation of everything —places, goods, processes— into exchange value, the *transformation into merchandise* of the world. How could we restore collective and vital rituals without new "myths", that is, without a new focus of values, perceptions, affections?

A ritual is a gesture that activates a certain energy, breathing new life into it. Without myth, rituals are hollow, bark without sap. We get together, we go through a series of gestures, *but nothing happens*. A Christmas dinner with strangers. Ritual without myth is the familiar that becomes hostile or threatening: the "sinister", according to Freud. Where there was once life and energy, only façades remain. All the current claims to "return to traditional values" contain something *sinister* within them.

TRANSFORMATION PRACTICES

Without rituals, we cannot feel part of something larger than ourselves, there is no transmission between generations. I agree with Han on this point. The problem is that if we come from a melancholic place, ritual is seen as *reactionary*, pitting the home against the storm, community to individuality, belonging to discontinuity, repetition to difference, familiarity to strangeness, sameness to otherness, meaning to nonsense, orientation to disorientation. It's a *conservative* view of forms.

Forms are those that allow us to inscribe vital phenomena (loves, passions, beliefs) in time and in the world. These vital phenomena, however, don't simply have to be conserved, but *renewed*. Forms are fetishized when they are separated from serving the vital phenomena that demand to be renewed. Let's cast our minds to any official commemoration: the fetishized form repeats itself instead of renewing, the instituted closes in over the instituting, the known over the unknown, what has been done over what is to be done. It becomes bombastic, rhetorical, overcoded, closed and monological.

Ritual, conceived as an operation of *passage*, gives way to the translation of energies. It is a practice of transformation, of metamorphosis, of renewal. It does not oppose stability to insta-

bility, but gives an immanent shape to the movement that is living, to the alterity that is time.
Nor does it oppose the new or the ephemeral to
permanence and duration, but rather it opera-
tes around the "re" prefix: recreate, revitalize,
regenerate, remake, relaunch...

CELEBRATING, READING, HEALING

I have just read a collection of studies on Jewish
thought. How could the Jews, without a state or
homeland to which to retreat, in dispersion and
exile, persecuted everywhere, survive for millennia as a people? The practices that allowed
this are not conservative; in reality things are
only maintained through their transformation.

Consider the *Shabbat*, which rather than simply
celebrating a historical event, *updates* an aspect
of the messianic promise. Another temporality,
not conservative nor progressive: exploded. The
update does not close the past close in on the
future, but rather it sees past, present and future as simultaneous entities. That's the magic right there. To be contemporary with past events.

Let's consider the reading of holy books, such
as the Torah or the Talmud, where the ability to
interrogate the text and to allow oneself to be
questioned by it is allowed and encouraged: the
reader is activated. Thus, between the text and
the reader, a range of meanings opens up. Constant exegesis keeps the questioning capacity of
the scriptures alive. Because what is habitable is
not the fullness of meaning itself, but an *interval*.

Let's now consider psychoanalysis (a Jewish
science!), where "healing" is not a matter of
repair, but of *transformation*. A transformation
that passes through the "endangerment" of
the subject, both protected and unprotected,

A ritual is a gesture that activates a certain energy, breathing new life into it. Without myth, rituals are hollow, bark without sap.

losing control in the free association of ideas, yet sheltered. Psychoanalysis is a "ceremony", as anyone who has gone through it knows, that it is always the same and at the same time it is always different. Difference and repetition rolled into one.

NECESSARY MOURNING

Stacking (capitalist) reason with a tendency to dissolve against (conservative) reason with a tendency to preserve is like trying to square a circle. It's the trap the *old left* is stuck in. In melancholy, Freud explains, the subject is hooked to the spectre of what was and no longer is — a prisoner of the absent. It's about following through with the *mourning* ritual right to the end, giving it a farewell as it deserves (it was important to us at one point) as we open ourselves up once again to the present, *thus regenerating desire.* ▲

Ritual, conceived as an operation of passage, gives way to the translation of energies.

Photographs captured by Iris Wang during the 2021 Qingming Festival in Hong Kong. In this event, the ritual of burning paper reproductions of earthly goods, such as money or clothing, is a time-honoured tradition so as to offer them to the deceased. Over the last few years, more and more electronic and digital devices, such as smartphones, tablets, headphones or game consoles, have been incorporated into the offerings.

Text
Patri di Filippo

Images
**US Library of Congress
Archive / US Naval
Observatory Archive**

MY·DEAREST·PISCES

My dear Pisces. My dearest Pisces. Today you look somewhat stagnant. It's hard to think ahead when the present is so overwhelming. And more so for you, given that, in difficult situations, you tend to dilute yourself in stronger personalities and to go with the flow. Your challenge is to begin seeing your sensitivity and intuition as talents rather than obstacles. We all know that behind that distracted appearance there's a fish capable of lashing strongly with its tail. My dear Pisces, let me ask you this: do you recognise yourself in these words? Maybe it's what psychologists call the Forer effect. Or maybe it's true that tonight the stars dance only for you.

Astrology is nothing new. It's been with us for thousands of years in thousands of different forms and, far from what it might seem, its separation from the scientific field of astronomy took place just a couple of centuries ago. The first astrological column in a newspaper dates from 1930, when *The Sunday Express* commissioned the astrologer R.H. Naylor to write a prediction of what the stars would bring to the newborn Princess Margaret. The unexpected success of the prediction was such that the newspaper made Naylor's column and his horoscopes a regular section. More recently, in the 60s and 70s, the New Age movement was accompanied by a significant amount of zodiac fever, with that spiritual rebirth symbolised by the entry into the age of Aquarius. But, after a few decades in which astrology had been relegated to women's magazines and Linda Goodman books (that no one remembers buying) on the shelves of every home, today references to the zodiac are everywhere. Where we were used to seeing traditional newspaper sections offering daily horoscopes to readers, we now have apps such as Co-Star or The Pattern offering AI generated horoscopes for each individual user, not to mention Twitter and Instagram accounts such as @astropoets, @notallgeminis or @charcastrology. Even the question "What sign are you?" seems to have superseded "What do you do for a living?" as the opener in a modern conversation. As of 2014, Google searches for keywords such as "horoscope", "astral chart" or "astrology" have only increased, reaching their peak in mid-2020 and doubling in number compared to 2004. At the end of last year, Zara launched a collection of scarves inspired by the zodiac, Tiffany & Co sells pendants of your sign for 300 euros, Amazon Prime recommends products to its subscribers based on their birth chart and even Nike launched together with Neymar a special edition of boots with the Constellation of the South printed on them. Is there more convincing proof that something has become extremely popular than when it becomes a niche market in its own right and all brands fall over themselves to jump on the bandwagon? However, although the raw material of astrology has remained the same for thousands of years, what *has* radically changed is the way we consume it and the forms it has taken. We may not all read our weekly horoscope, but we've all Liked a post such as, "What Game of Thrones character are you according to your sign?" (or most of us anyway: more on that later). As journalist Amanda Hess pointed out in *How Astrology Took Over The Internet*, lifelong astrology is perfect for the new dynamic of the Internet: it provides an easy framework for infinitely personalised material, it's aimed at young people and women, and has just the right touch of nostalgia. "It's the Cosmic Buzzfeed test", she writes.

> Is there more convincing proof that something has become extremely popular than when it becomes a niche market in its own right and all brands fall over themselves to jump on the bandwagon?

For Andrea Gumes, journalist, presenter of *Tardeo* on Radio Primavera Sound and author of the horoscopes for Vogue Spain magazine, "the current success enjoyed by horoscopes is not so much because of the prediction of the future based on the stars as it is the sense of community that it contributes. The whole meeting another Virgo and thinking 'ah, we're both obsessed with order'". And if there's something that perfectly sublimates these identification and community dynamics, it's a meme. This is also seen by Charas Vega, better known on Instagram as Charcastrology, an account with almost 60,000 followers that interprets the zodiac through nostalgic PowerPoint aesthetics and relates them to topics as diverse as Temptation Island, an El Bosco painting or pop songs. "The meme format is all-encompassing," she claims. "It's a new canvas that allows complex ideas to be transferred to simple graphic representations, with an added humour component. So astrology jumped on the bandwagon". Because astrology is not merely knowing the twelve solar signs. There is a whole world of conjunctions, planetary transits,

rulerships, houses and quadrants in which each position of one or another planet has significant influences. Having said that, it's a relatively simple system that allows us to express complex ideas about personalities, life cycles or experiences of

each one through easily recognisable symbolic representations. This symbolic representation, therefore, works like a dream on the web, and is effective in another symbol system of symbols: memes.

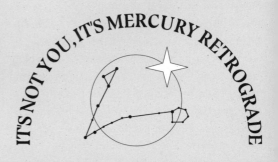

IT'S NOT YOU, IT'S MERCURY RETROGRADE

"More than wondering about the phenomenon itself," says Andrea, "we should look at what variables have occurred for everything to converge in this need to be part of something to which horoscopes have been able to respond". Which brings us back to 1930, to that first horoscope of Princess Margaret that appeared at a time when the catastrophic echoes of the crash of 29 still reverberated throughout society. And to the era of Aquarius predicted by the New Age, which symbolised leaving the dark age of Pisces —marked by wars, conflicts and various misfortunes— to enter a global, astrological haven of peace. As then, we are now also living in a time marked by instability and uncertainty. In particular young people, who unsurprisingly are those who consume the most astrology. We are children of the 2008 crisis and job insecurity, political instability, lack of trust in democratic institutions and the resurgence of far-right discourse, among others. And, to top it all, a global pandemic comes along and wreaks havoc across all areas of our lives: economic, social, as well as physical and mental health. It doesn't take an astrologer to know that our future looks rather mediocre.

"We are biased towards optimism and predictability because we cannot bear the idea of arbitrariness. We tend to see the world as more predictable and fair than it really is, and when it is not, it affects our mood. In moments in which the uncertainty of reality becomes evident, we are more motivated than ever to counteract that sense of vertigo with clear explanations, whatever they may be", explains Fernando Blanco, Social Psychologist specialised in contingencies, causality and thoughts considered irrational within human learning. Furthermore, human beings are eminently narrative creatures: we explain our existence by intertwining past, present and future through causal and objective relationships, and we live our experience in the world through signs and meanings. In the midst of this physical, political and emotional earthquake, astrology provides a meaning, a purpose. Horoscopes offer us explanations of why everything

> Lifelong astrology is perfect for the new dynamic of the Internet: it provides an easy framework for infinitely personalised material, it's aimed at young people and women, and has just the right touch of nostalgia.

seems to go wrong for us today, and the promise that tomorrow will be just that little bit better. They encourage us to look within ourselves to find the strength to move forward. Both Andrea and Charas say, in fact, that they began to be interested in the horoscope at a time of crisis. Andrea had been fired, and Charas was heartbroken by a Scorpio.

But physics also provides certainties, and I don't see anyone wearing an "I am Newton's Third Law ♥" t-shirt, just like there are plenty of people wearing

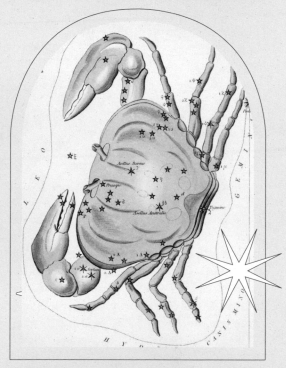

their zodiac sign. If we're supposed to be rational beings, why do we look for explanations in models that are not supported by evidence such as horoscopes (but also conspiracy theories, fake news or UFO sightings)? "The key to understanding this duality is to realise that reasoning correctly requires effort and time. That's why we have automatic mechanisms, known in psychology as 'heuristics', which work with very few resources and without the need to pay too much attention," says Fernando. The problem is that, although these mechanisms almost always work, sometimes they make mistakes. And when they do, it's always in the same direction. They're systematic. "There are many types of heuristics that, together, help us understand beliefs such as the horoscope. For example, we have confirmation bias, which we

are sufficient vague enough to encompass anyone. "By presenting us with an ambiguous description, we have the opportunity to interpret it in different ways, and we prefer the interpretation that reinforce our pre-existing beliefs, our starting point," explains Fernando. This is especially the case if in these descriptions there is a predominance of positive affirmations, since "the vast majority of people see themselves as honest, benevolent and just".

But if there is also an egocentric component in our tendency towards horoscopes, how do we explain that 21st century astrology works precisely because of its community spirit? For Fernando, it's a matter of "often, beliefs —both irrational and not— are used to bring social groups together. If you want to belong to a group and take advantage of its protection and support, you have to validate all the beliefs that shape it. This is how we often uncritically acquire many unfounded beliefs, almost by cultural transmission and by placing trust in our equals".

use to hold beliefs even though there is clear evidence to challenge them". You know, that person I met the other night in a bar never replies to my messages, they don't look at my Instagram stories, they don't call me, but it's not that they're ignoring me, it's just that they're really busy. In the field of horoscopes, for Fernando this would be: "instead of 'I argue a lot, even when the horoscope tells me I'll have a good day', we interpret it as, 'the horoscope told me that today I would have bad luck, and I just had an argument'. "Another mechanism could be the so-called 'hindsight bias,'" he argues. "I call it the 'I knew that already' effect: once we've known the outcome of something, we can't help but think that (a) the outcome was predictable and inevitable, and (b) we already knew that outcome was going to happen." I've had a dreadful day: I got fired, I broke up with my boyfriend and I was struck by lightning. But my horoscope already told me so: we're under Mercury retrograde.

The fact that the horoscope seems written especially for you can also be explained in psychology through the so-called Forer effect, according to which we tend to accept as valid affirmations that seem to be tailor-made to us but that, in reality,

GREAT EVILS, PETIT BOURGEOIS REMEDIES?

Roland Barthes wrote in his *Mythologies* that "astrology is the literature of the petit bourgeoisie," referring to that kind of literature that "in its degraded forms, never goes beyond talking about what has already been lived," in which writing doesn't

pose a question, but rather it reinforces reality, the established order. Barthes is attacking the weekly horoscopes of *Elle* magazine, considering them a mere reproduction of the petty bourgeoisie and its worldly concerns (the family home, matters of the heart, friendships) in which destiny's temporal unit coincides, surprise surprise, with the working week, an approach that's not lost on modern-day fortune-tellers. Andrea herself confesses that she has often wondered from what privilege point she writes her horoscopes. "What right do I have to say that such a sign will take a trip or see a big change in their work life, if right now we're seeing ski-high unemployment?" she says. However, and against

Barthes, the fact that horoscopes can function as a hobby for those who are already comfortable and successful in life doesn't exclude the fact that they are also a playful and literary way to promote more inclusive visions of reality and subvert established myths, like romantic love or toxic masculinity. It would be unfair to say that today's horoscopes are the same as the ones we could have read in an *Elle* from the 60s. "When writing, I keep inclusive language in mind, especially in terms of gender and

sexuality. I don't like saying that sign X is going to find a boyfriend, and it would never occur to me to write, 'this month you will get pregnant', as Susan Miller could do. I prefer to talk about couples in the plural, for example, and, in general, use language and situations with which anyone can identify",

> In moments in which the uncertainty of reality becomes evident, we are more motivated than ever to counteract that sense of vertigo with clear explanations, whatever they may be.

Andrea continues. "Astrology also makes us explore feelings that don't always have a place in our daily conversations, such as our weaknesses, trauma, loss, self-sabotage, victimisation... Far from being a mere self-indulgent mechanism, it also forces us to face aspects of ourselves that are uncomfortable." "This introspection and capacity for self-analysis very much clashes with the values of toxic masculinity, in which talking about one's own feelings and fears is seen as a weakness", says Charas, reflecting on why astrology has so little acceptance in cis and heterosexual men. "Personally, it has helped me as a tool to share very personal and complicated issues with others, starting conversations that, perhaps, if it weren't for astrology, I would never have started, since I don't usually go around asking people about their traumas," she concludes. "Being able to share with someone something that has happened to you or that you feel... for me that's the most beautiful part," adds Andrea. "In an increasingly individualistic and atomised world, I think we have been quite skil-

> It would be unfair to say that today's horoscopes are the same as the ones we could have read in an *Elle* from the 60s.

FOR A LITTLE COSMIC LOVE

ful in creating a space and a community of women. I don't ban men from the community, nor do I particularly care whether or not they read the horoscope, but I address female readers because women are my safe space, my community".

Be that as it may, there is a huge difference between writing a horoscope in a magazine or creating a meme about how wicked Scorpios are and cleaning chakras for 200 euros an hour or keeping on the phone a lady who has just divorced for the small price of 6 euros/minute. What's wrong with talking about your own feelings, getting to know yourself better and connecting with others, be it through astrology or in a bar with a couple of beers? In the end, just like in the Los Romeos song, everything we do is for a little bit, just a little bit, of love.

If you ask me, the truth is that I'm not interested in whether the horoscope is real or if people really believe in it, much less making value judgments. But I will say this: in the act of looking up at the night sky and wanting to believe that therein lie all the answers, I don't see stupidity, but rather tenderness. We have been on this Earth for millions of years, the result of a coincidence of cosmic proportions, and we still have no idea why we're here. So we looked up at the same sky that catapulted us to this hostile place with no instructions nor anyone to ask for guidance, and we sought explanations. In a way, we deserve them. We look up at the sky and, although we know that we're nothing more than an insignificant blue dot in an ocean of constellations, tonight the stars dance only for us. ▲

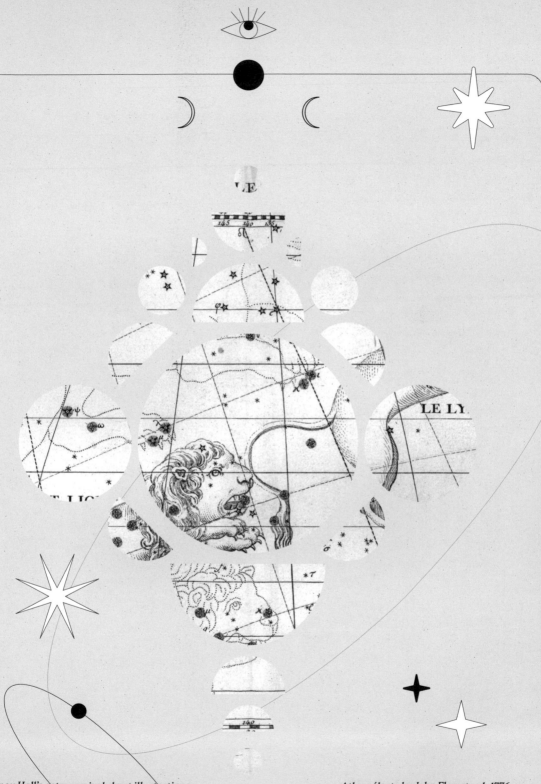

Sidney Hall's astronomical chart illustrations,
circa 1831. US Library of Congress.

Atlas céleste by John Flamsteed, 1776.
United States Naval Observatory.

REMINDERS   Now
ZOOM - Entrepreneurship Conference

Text
Luis Herrero

Images
La Nueva Carne

THE ADVENT OF THE GURU

Separated from one another by the ethereal wall that the internet raises between us, viral isolation and the precariousness of remote working relationships have turned us into fresh meat for the preacher. Only now they wear a suit jacket, and what once were parables of transcendence and communion are now parables on success, resilience and the beautiful art of "being your own boss".

An acquaintance of the present author, who we're calling M for now, came across an ad for a promising online business school. With a modern and well-laid out design, youthful language and catchy slogans, its website differs little from that of a typical start-up. The school's main attraction lies in promising exciting trips and encounters around the world, something open, according to the company's founder, to those known as *digital nomads*. This concept is, in principle, merely descriptive: it refers to a remote employee, that is, someone who works online without having to physically commute to an office. However, and unlike what happens with conventional technical training, the knowledge or skills which this course claims to provide its stu-

The internet and new technologies have provided gurus and pseudo-therapists with the optimal environment for seducing us with unlimited promises of personal and material satisfaction.

dents with consist, again according to the founder, in "accessing the collective intelligence that is behind all my achievements", or in "unlocking your inner self, because everything you do is born from you", and in overcoming formative stages known as the "health clover" or the "money magnet". Before long, M found herself talking about her training in terms of "personal introspection", how "we are our own limit", or explaining the importance of "taking fear out of the equation". And let's not forget the fact that we're talking about a school offering classes in web design, online advertising and digital writing and which, at the same time, promises its students access to "a parallel world where you are nobody, where you have no attachment to what you've achieved and what you haven't".

What I've just described is merely one of the more refined examples of how the internet and new technologies have provided gurus and pseudo-therapists with the optimal environment for seducing us with unlimited promises of personal and material satisfaction. In this case, the value proposition stems from our unconscious association between "our dream job and Christian salvation: the idea that, once I have achieved my ultimate work goals, I will finally be happy and live in a parallel ontological plane in which the passage of time, worries, corruption and death simply don't exist," according to philosopher and doctor in Cultural Anthropology Iñaki Domínguez in his book *Sociología del moderneo* (2017). These new gurus combine the key features of hippie culture —expansion of consciousness, anti-establishment or anti-herd rebellion— and of yuppies, those young high-level professionals who value independence —both

financial and social— over and above almost any other consideration.

Etymologically, the Sanskrit word "guru" means "spiritual master": in the Upanishad it is presented as the "dispeller of darkness." This ancient concept underwent a resurgence during the sixties, a period in which counterculture gave birth to the most varied mix of techniques to promote personal or spiritual rebirth, as well as a colourful group of leaders who presented themselves as qualified for this task. From Ken Kesey, one of the greatest pontiffs of psychedelics, to Osho, self-proclaimed spiritual leader known as the "sex guru", or even the notorious Charles Manson, these guides filled the religious and philosophical void of young people of an entire generation. Those most critical of this new spirituality saw in it nothing but a vicarious or degraded form of religion —following the adage, erroneously attributed to Chesterton, according to which when human beings no longer believe in God it's not because they've stopped believing in anything, but because they believe in everything— and it could be said that our contemporary society has a perverted version of those mystical idealisms of half a century ago.

The paradigm of these times can be found in the figure of Betinho Massaro, a self-proclaimed spiritual teacher whose fame is due largely to the internet. What sets Massaro apart from other countercultural gurus is his explicit goal of presenting his teachings "in such a way that they can be integrated into the different axes of our society"; that is to say, his doctrine accommodates the dominant forms of thought and, a priori, requires

MOSES PLEADING WITH ISRAEL

Deut. 6:1-19.

GOLDEN TEXT:—Beware lest thou forget the Lord.
Deut. 6:12.

moses-pleading.jpg

"The coach would be a substitute for that older brother who teaches you how to live your life, or a new kind of priest, integrating you into the system through the values of dominant neoliberalism." — Iñaki Domínguez

no personal sacrifice. He defines himself as a "civilization enhancer," no less, who spreads his ideas of personal growth through an online university —Trinfinity Academy— that promises free access to "more than 800 hours and 400 videos of Betinho's retreats and recordings of his conferences". He also talks about himself using terms like "entrepreneur" and "investor," and celebrates the dynamics of the business world with a frankness that would have been unthinkable in his predecessors decades ago.

When the fear of sects took hold in the US, the image of these groups and their acolytes consisted of large agglomerations of people physically gathered around a leader, celebrating orgiastic rituals and consuming narcotics. This stereotype, not necessarily based on reality, is being progressively replaced by that of the isolated individual who jumps from course to course on spirituality or personal growth like a squirrel from tree to tree, sitting at his computer and without the need to experience any direct human contact whatsoever. And today's students are often seduced by goals that are all-encompassing and, therefore, contradictory: idealistic self-realization, on the one hand, and earthly economic or social benefits, on the other. The perfect fusion of hippie and yuppie.

THE DEMATERIALISATION OF THERAPY

The challenges of meeting in person since the beginning of the pandemic has spurred the market for online courses, based on recorded lectures, video conferences and downloadable study materials. The coaching industry has been no exception,

and a plethora of tutor-led self-help and personal growth courses are advertised on the web. Through a series of searches —Facebook groups or Meetup meetings are fertile ground— I came across courses advertised under names such as "Contact your angels and redesign your life", therapists who present themselves as experts in disciplines such as "Holistic Emotional Therapy" or "Inner Child Healing", or with coaches whose courses are advertised under slogans such as "You are the universe". In most cases, the same therapist offered a wide range of courses at low prices —anything from €30 to €80— or offered a first class free of charge, usually via videoconference.

"Nowadays you get more than the offer to see everything in a lovely pink light: you can also generate false realities through technology, which is already the beginning of the Matrix", explains Iñaki Domínguez. "In that world, COVID-19 doesn't exist, no one exploits you, and from there it's a small step to full-on virtual reality, that image in which you are sitting at your computer on which limitless memes have been based. Your window to the world consists in a world of representations: you could perfectly well dispense with the real world in favour of courses that create tailor-made representations."

For the therapist and psychological adviser Adriana Royo, three factors influence the popularity of these virtual on-demand courses: "the first key element is the elimination of any kind of effort: I don't want to leave home, but I want to receive therapy easily and quickly, like masturbation. The second is the infantilisation of society, which leads to reflective deficiencies that turn us into children desperately in need of external guidance. The third is our self-image, which we want to strengthen but without going through any process involving deep thought: most users simply want to come out of their therapy sessions feeling better straight away."

ANATOMY OF A NEW GURU

In his book *How to Hammer Happiness into us: An Anti-Self Help Manual*, Domínguez traces the origins of self-help to ancient Greece and the Stoic philosophers. We don't need too much imagination to see Socrates as a predecessor of today's coaches. "It's to do with the figure of the pastor, someone who accompanies you and guides you on your path. Psychoanalysis talks of this replacing the confessional and the priests of the past. Now, bereft of any traditional dogmas, people need that figure to show them how to move around in the world. The coach would be a substitute for that older brother who teaches you how to live your life, or a new kind of priest, integrating you into the system through the values of dominant neoliberalism," explains Iñaki.

In other cases, gurus use the absence of reference points of their clientele to serve them a rehashed philosophy with a vaguely Oriental stamp. Swallowing is always easier when the diner lacks education or a coherent value system, as shown by the following case explained by Adriana Royo: "I remember a patient who came to me with severe depression, and they explained to me that they had spent the last two years following a YouTuber who taught Advaita Vedanta classes —a non-dualistic school of Hindu philosophy— in which they explain that there is no duality, that is, there is neither good

nor evil, night or day, and that one must transcend this false dichotomy. And for two years the patient tried to live according to these teachings, based on prescribing humility and modesty, on apologising for everything… and the patient came to me with a severe depression that shocked me, but they said they had no right to be angry because duality didn't exist."

The biggest problem with coaching lies in its ambiguity. A coach is not a psychologist —although they may be trained in psychology— nor are they a spiritual guide, but often in their persona the boundaries between the two disciplines are blurred. Frequently, the proclamations of high-profile members of the community adopt a salvific tone, vaguely inspired by the speeches of American preachers: they demand the client's total commitment and admit no questioning of their techniques: "The level of dependence that

Idealistic self-realization, on the one hand, and earthly economic or social benefits, on the other. The perfect fusion of hippie and yuppie.

some professionals create is huge, when in reality all they're seeing is a potential wallet to drain, and they often target narcissistic people with a need for external power because they lack such power within themselves. A good coach should accompany you in such a way that *you* are the one to find the

best solution, and they won't generate a dynamic of dependency. In that accompaniment there is always an element of uncertainty: the coach does not have the power to save the client or fix their problems, they can't have the pride to believe such a thing," explains Adriana.

VICTIM OR PERPETRATOR?

As in the case of pyramid scams —in which maintaining the ruse depends on each unsuspecting member attracting new victims— many of those

Never before have we had such a profusion of examples of personal fulfilment —whether genuine or not— seemingly created from scratch.

duped by a guru or coach spread the virtues of their conversion to others, who go on to join the coach's client portfolio. And, unlike the case of purely financial frauds, the victim has a greater incentive to become a perpetrator: not only is their money at stake, but also, more worryingly, their ego.

"We're afraid of being rejected, and we build out our character to be liked. When a therapist or a guru confronts someone they run the risk of the client getting upset, which is why many will never do it —what they will do however is mollycoddle," says Royo. That massaged ego grows like a snowball thrown down the slope, and at some point, al-

though doubt will start to take hold, few people will be willing to accept that it's all just a big lie. That's when they won't want to be alone in the deception and will attempt to attract new followers to provide them with emotional reinforcement and convince them that they are in fact on the right track. This can be seen in the testimonies that the Spanish YouTuber and investigative journalist Tamayo collect on his channel: one of their great assets is the skill with which they show how tenuous the line is that separates victim from perpetrator, and how the perpetrators are not always cynics.

What's more, the Internet provides us with an illusion of the democratisation of success. Never before have we had such a profusion of examples of personal fulfilment —whether genuine or not— seemingly created from scratch. With little relation to traditional professions and as volatile as a Bitcoin, the avenues to make a fortune are more appealing than ever, and personal gratification is just around the corner. Iñaki Domínguez thus summarises the kind of anchoring in reality required to avoid the song of the sirens: "What we need is to relate to the world and invite ourselves to listen to others; that is an attitude that is hardly ever cultivated, and some therapists out there don't encourage you to listen and to experiment, but rather to listen to yourself and engage in massive doses of introspection, instead of learning from the objective world. In the end, what helps people mature is venturing into that world of objects, humiliating themselves and becoming adults. The alternative turns us neurotic, only believing our inner discourses and only being guided by their own story." ▲

THE SECULAR

OF

Images
Mario Domingos

Text
Sergio Parra

RELIGION

IMMORTALITY

Achieving immortality would be, for many, the human race's definitive symbol of progress. Editing our genome to avoid ageing, turning our consciousness into new media, exploring therapeutic cloning or living eternally in the metaverse: the range of options we have in front of us to achieve this might lead us to think that we are close to reaching our goal. However, beyond the practical barriers, already mighty difficult to overcome, there are even more complex ones that take us back to as yet unanswered ancestral questions.

Baseball legend Ted Williams; creator of TV comedy *The Facts of Life*, Dick Clair; Iranian futurist writer Fereidoun M. Esfandiary, are some of the cryonauts stored in Dewar flasks, gigantic thermos filled with liquid nitrogen in the facilities of Alcor Life Extension Foundation, in Scottsdale, Arizona. All were cryonised just after death, waiting to wake up in a future where technology allows the thawing and cure of humanity's most universal disease: death.

Many of the transhumanist ideologues sound more like priests than scientists.

Alcor is just one of many examples, adorned with technological elements, of the ancestral desire of human beings to stop decrepitude and death. The central theme of *The Epic of Gilgamesh*, considered the oldest known epic work, is the search for immortality: "At the bottom of the sea there is a plant similar to the thorny lycia, it pricks like a rose bush, and hurts the hands; if your fingers grasp it, you will possess immortality!"

Humanity's determination to extend life as much as possible also underlies various Greek myths, such as the wish that the Cumaean Sibyl granted to Apollo: you will live as many years as the number of grains of sand you are able to grasp with your hand. But sand, of course, tends to slip through the fingers.

Later, through technology, it was argued that we could not only create human-like machines, but also enhance ourselves because, essentially, we are also similar to machines, as suggested by René Descartes' *Treatise on Man*: "We see clocks, artificial sources, mills and other similar machines that, despite being made only by men, have the ability to move by themselves in various ways."

Despite its Promethean resonances (whose fateful conclusion we are already aware of), there's a handful of scientists and ideologues warning that we are about to achieve some kind of immortality, either within our own flesh, through cybernetic implants or by transferring our consciousness to long strings of zeros and ones. Particularly optimistic are the proselytes of transhumanism, which establishes that the next evolutionary link will not be natural, but catalysed by new technologies through two approaches: (1) lengthening life by delaying aging, finding the key to rescind the body's expiration date, something like a button that stops natural aging, and (2) dispensing with the limitations of the body altogether. Since the mind is made up of nothing more than information, it could be downloaded and transferred to other bodies, even to other media, as if it were a computer system.

The priests of transhumanism hide behind new technologies that seem to be extracted directly from a science fiction movie: precision medicine, gene editing, cybernetics, bioprinting, or brain-computer interfaces.

NEW PRIESTS

Just 150 years ago, only 20% of people reached the age of seventy. Now, in any developed country, 80% of citizens exceed that age. This is one of many arguments wielded by guru- or priest-like visionaries (Rasputin beard included), such as biomedical gerontologist Aubrey de Gray and his TED talks, or his book *Ending Aging*.

But does the fact that we have increased life expectancy necessarily mean that we can increase it even more? To achieve this, the priests of transhumanism hide behind new technologies that seem to be extracted directly from a science fiction movie: precision medicine, gene editing, cybernetics, bioprinting, or brain-computer interfaces.

Thus, among the projects that are underway to achieve some kind of immortality, we find a wide range, going from the moderately plausible to the fanciful, such as Dmitry Itskov's *Avatar Project* (copying the brain onto a computer format thanks to advances such as the *Human Brain Project*, whose aim is to simulate the functions of the brain's over eighty-six billion neurons), Google's Alphabet division (synthetic biology, virtual immortality and optogenetics), Human Longevity Inc. (genetic databases to find the keys to longevity), Kronos Longevity Research Institute (stem cells, therapeutic cloning), Palo Alto Longevity Prize (a financial award created by Joon Yun, hedge fund manager, given to anyone who breaks the code of life and cures the aging), among others.

If DNA is our body's set of instructions, then perhaps editing it would be enough so that we are simply not doomed to age.

But the transhumanist movement is also full of charlatans. We don't need to ascribe to techno-scepticism or even Luddism to question some of the risky assertions of these digital utopians. Many of the transhumanist ideologues sound more like priests than scientists, such as Max More, philosopher, futurologist and founder of the Extropy Institute, or Natasha Vita-More, author of the *Transhuman Manifesto* and the *Declaration of the Transhumanist Arts*.

Technologically speaking, it seems that the simplest way to increase longevity and, eventually, achieve immortality is to prevent our body from deteriorating over time, by slowing down or even stopping the ticking of the cellular clock. If DNA is our body's set of instructions, then perhaps editing it would be enough so that we are simply not doomed to age. However, the baseline problem is that we are dealing with a machine that exceeds any other in complexity and all the scientists who have had a crack at it have invariably felt like Dorian Gray.

Furthermore, it's not enough to merely edit the human genome. For starters, the genome is much more complex than we originally believed and, in addition, each genome is unique and changes continually as it interacts with the environment.

As if all this weren't enough, the genome (all genetic material) is not the Book of Life itself but the tip of the iceberg, the cover of a book with many pages. Pages like the metabolome (all hormones and other metabolites), the proteome (all proteins), the microbiome (all microbes), the connectome (all neural connections). And all those pages also interact with each other, and with the book cover. In short, layers upon layers that feed into one another and remind us that the more we know about the body, the more we realise how little we know. Thus, despite all the achievements in recent years, Gattaca is still a long way off.

FROM ATOM TO BIT

We could forget about most of this complexity and focus on just one organ: our brain. After all, that's where our consciousness seems to reside. Wouldn't it be easier to translate the myriad neurons in our brain into bits so that they live forever in a computer?

The problem is that, even if we confine ourselves to a single organ of our body, we still face enormous complexity, a complexity covered with philosophical thorns as prickly as Gilgamesh's own lycia.

An iPhone and a human body are made up of the same elements on the periodic table, only arranged in a different way.

The complexity of the brain doesn't come so much from the number of neurons, which is enormous, but from the way in which they connect with each other, the so-called connec-

tome. If in the 1,400 grams of gelatinous brain there are between ten thousand and one hundred thousand million neurons, each neuron, in turn, establishes between five thousand and fifty thousand connections with neighbouring neurons. Mapping a connectome would mean precisely knowing the architecture of no less than a hundred trillion connections.

To create a database capable of housing the location of neurons, the dimensions and the arrangements of axons, dendrites and synapses, requires not only a huge capacity for data storage and processing, but also a tool capable of scanning a brain at very high resolution, as new technology analyst Mark O'Connell warns in *To Be a Machine*: "What would it mean to extract information from that substrate to transpose it to some other medium? Would the information have any meaning outside its original context?"

Nature's code doesn't seem inscrutable to us, which is why initiatives such as the *Human Brain Project* were born, led by neuroscientist Henry Markram and powered by more than one billion euros from the European Union. The purpose is to develop a functional model of the human brain so that it can be simulated in a supercomputer using artificial neural networks.

However, can we be sure that we know enough about our consciousness to reproduce it? Is it enough to merely imitate its processes? Isn't some nuance lost in that imitation, in that translation and extrapolation?

The proposal, in principle, seems reasonable: if we are already capable of manufacturing objects as complex as an iPhone, what prevents us from dreaming of the idea that one day we can disassemble and reassemble our bodies and our minds? An iPhone and a human body are made up of the same elements on the periodic table, only arranged in a different way. As early as 1655, philosopher Thomas Hobbes wrote in *De Corpore*: "By reasoning I understand computation."

However, although we might accept that the brain is just an information processor, a computer, we forget that it is constantly reorganising itself based on the experiences it receives through the body's senses. Each stimulus received through sight or touch, for example, triggers changes not only in the brain, but in other organs, such as the stomach, which in turn influences the brain (95% of all the serotonin that runs through our body is found in the intestine). If there is no such continuous reorganisation as a result of the inputs, feedback and interrelation with the other organs (or we do not know how to imitate it completely), does consciousness also emerge? What's the use of living in the Matrix if it's not really us who are there?

WHAT ARE WE?

Given the enormous conceptual and epistemological challenge we face, the most optimistic technologists who aspire to achieve immortality attempt to summarise consciousness as the ability to have subjective experiences (although there is still room to philosophise a little more until we pin down how we can be so sure that a Roomba vacuum cleaner doesn't have subjective experiences). This, then, would be what would distinguish us from the rest of the matter in the universe, be it 1.0 or 2.0.

The most optimistic technologists who aspire to achieve immortality attempt to summarise consciousness as the ability to have subjective experiences.

To resolve whether our digital or analogue copy has subjective experiences, technologists ignore tough questions such as whether consciousness exists in itself and is located in our body, and focus on what can be experimentally verified: how the brain processes information at the computational level. Or to put it another way: the only thing we know for sure is that we are conscious. That is, if we can perfectly recreate the functioning of our brain, we must admit that this copy of us is conscious and that, eventually, it is us. It's an assumption, yes, but so it is that we ourselves are conscious, in a way.

To scrutinise our level of consciousness, we have techniques for exploring and monitoring our brain such as electroencephalography (EEG) or magnetoencephalography (MEG), in addition to the powerful and functional Magnetic Resonance Imaging (fMRI), capable of creating a three-dimensional map of the brain every second with a resolution of the order of one millimetre, or invasive electrocorticography (ECoG), which consists of placing a hundred wires on the surface of the brain tissue itself, or electrophysiology, which inserts micro-wires into said tissue, sometimes finer than a human hair, to register voltages of up to a thousand points simultaneously.

Summed up in simple terms: if the brain lights up like a Christmas tree, then it is working properly and it is conscious. If we can extrapolate an exact neurobiological correlate in a digital or analogue copy, then, we can affirm that this correlate is not only alive, but also conscious. Therefore, this approach to the theory of consciousness would be similar to that of, for example, Newton's theory of gravity: it allows us to check repeatedly that it works, that the same results are always produced after applying the same changes.

> *If we can extrapolate an exact neurobiological correlate in a digital or analogue copy, then, we can affirm that this correlate is not only alive, but also conscious.*

Ironically, this vision of things is in itself contradictory: on the one hand it conceptualises the mind as a simple emergent property of the interactions between physical objects, but simultaneously it is affirmed that mind and matter can be separated or translated into another format: "In other words, it manifests itself as a new form of dualism, even as a kind of mysticism", O'Connell warns.

Of course, we can ignore the philosophical background and trust that we will not die when we are copied onto a computer. But in doing so we not only indulge in a new kind of faith, but we also overlook all associated bioethical problems. We ignore a reflection that is reminiscent of the bitter debates about abortion or euthanasia, only too technically difficult for lay people to understand. Which, in turn, can lead to individual and collective decisions on cultures and religions that will cause unfathomable social and economic dislocations: people who will live many more years or who will reside in a digital paradise because their purchasing power or their morals allow it in contrast to people with a low life expectancy or worse, made of flesh and blood. Which in turn, like matryoshka dolls, will fuel the flourishing of new socio-economic and moral problems. And right in the centre, at the core, the great question of all, the one that has plagued humanity since the first philosophical babbling: nothing less than the meaning of human existence. ▲

GAIA, OR THE GODDESS OF THE ANTHRO-POCENE

Text
Enrique Rey

Images
Miren Pastor

Let's suppose, for a moment, that we're travelling in a damaged submarine, that we're in a nuclear power plant about to explode, that an avalanche is upon us. We immediately experience a moment of despair or heroism, or we come to the idea of digging a hole in the snow with our hands. But just before that (it's almost an action movie cliché, oddly enough also to be found in Borges' *The Secret Miracle*) there may be time to organise a few ideas, recap and spare a thought for our loved ones, or even to experience enlightenment enabling us to finally realise who we are (or who we *were*).

This is the situation many contemporary philosophers and scientists find themselves in. And there's consensus: climate change is now unstoppable and its consequences will be traumatic. What is being debated today would be scandalous if it weren't for the fact that we've been reading about it for years, without so much as a flinch —I'm writing about it right now, in fact, while listening to the noise of the dryer in the background: how many joules of energy is it consuming, I wonder? What's being debated is whether it's desirable for human civilisation to collapse sooner or later (in the latter case, the consequences will be all the worse), what sacrifices are we passing on to how many future generations and if, ultimately, there is a future (what kind of future and on which planet?) for the human race and the vast wealth of culture that it has created over millennia.

These issues transcend the fields of ecology or geology and bleed well into anthropology, but they soon transcend even that. We're living at a time of both emergency and emergence of new speculative currents that aim to respond to the colossal challenges posed by the climate crisis. Perhaps the majority of the global population is like a deer paralysed in the headlights of an approaching car: either because it doesn't believe in the solidity of the bumper, or because it doesn't understand what the bright light actually is. In opposition to this, or in an attempt to explain this apathy, some thinkers are devising stories, metaphors —I've used a few in just three paragraphs— and even contemporary myths. The climate crisis is also the crisis of Modernity and, since we've ended up here thanks to Modernity's way of thinking (the idea that humans can overcome any obstacle through reason and technique), alternative systems of thought crop up and are recovered (critics and their well-worn, widely accepted dogmas, such as the incompatibility between scientific fact and personal opinion), or which retrieve and re-assess indigenous religions. Since the era of idealism ends with our possible extinction, perhaps the way to save it (or at least to come to terms with it, before its arrival) requires irrationality and the creation of new shared fictions. Isn't that what religions are in the first place?

THE ANTHROPOCENE, LIVING IN AN EXPERIMENT THAT'S OUT OF CONTROL

During a congress in February 2000, Paul Crutzen, an unassuming chemist —as unassuming as a Nobel Prize Laureate can be— felt a rush of inspiration and, interrupting a colleague's speech, exclaimed, "We no longer live in the Holocene... we live in the Anthropocene!" Crutzen could never have imagined that this happy occurrence, the term which summarised so many things (humanity's total impact on Earth) and at the same time evaluated their scope (he placed that impact at the level that the scientific community uses to mark the boundary between one geological era and another) would become, a couple of decades later, the word of the day. In 2020 the Canadian singer Grimes, an international popstar, released the album *Miss Anthropocene*, leaving no doubt that best-selling novels and poetry collections on the subject are just around the corner.

> The climate crisis is also the crisis of Modernity and, since we've ended up here thanks to Modernity's way of thinking, alternative systems of thought crop up and are recovered.

And for good reason. When researchers across different fields combined their data, they realised that, especially since the "Great Acceleration" of the second half of the 20th century, humanity —and this has been confirmed by different stratigraphic and biological markers— had become the main agent responsible for the changes seen across the planet. Perhaps the best way to see to what extent our collective behaviour in recent decades has been exceptional is to measure the energy we have consumed and continue to consume (according to basic physics, energy is the ability to perform work, and we seem to have worked particularly hard), and to reveal at what scale we're moving in right now. First, a couple of facts: humans during the 20th century used ten times more energy than the sum of all our ancestors during the immediately preceding millennium; and the energy that powers the world's devices every instant is around 18 TW, or approximately the equivalent of a tsunami or very large volcano, the difference being that our consumption is constant, rather than lasting a few minutes or hours. Our energy consumption has the magnitude of a perpetual earthquake.

The great paradox of the Anthropocene is that, precisely when us humans begin to be able to modify —involuntarily— the biological and geological processes of the planet we inhabit, that's when we lose control of our destiny: heirs of Frankenstein and Prometheus, we have triggered something we are unable to fully control. The Anthropocene positions us "face to face with the planet," in the words of Bruno Latour and, again according to the French philosopher, "forces us to re-evaluate what we previously called *natural* and what was previously called *cultural* or *human*." This is perhaps the most profound epistemological consequence of all these transformations: the reassuring distance that used to separate us from nature (which we understood simply as a landscape or something to observe under a microscope), and anthropocentrism (until recently we walked haughtily and lonely in a god-free world) breaks down. We have discovered —perhaps the pandemic is another sign of this?— that we are fatally connected to everything that surrounds us.

The most optimistic out there believe that soon we'll be able to free ourselves from all the ties that confine us to this exhausted planet and humanity will be, at last, free from the world. They believe that even more science and even more technology will lead us to the conquest of the Universe (with its potentially infinite resources) or even to the dematerialisation of consciousness (we can detach ourselves from our bodies and live forever as pure data: transhumanism's last frontier). But chances are that the devices capable of providing us with these utopias will never be developed or that, long before we can successfully design them, environmental catastrophes will have wiped us out completely. The Sixth Mass Extinction (the sixth in the history of Life and the only one caused by humans) is hot on our heels, its speed one hundred times faster than usual. Although it's difficult for our society of abundance to imagine a scenario similar to those that led to the extinction of other mammals (after all, their ecosystems disappeared because we folded them into our own ecosystem), there are many theorists who believe that a series of climatic and geological disasters could compromise the survival of practically all the individuals of our species (and at this point, the

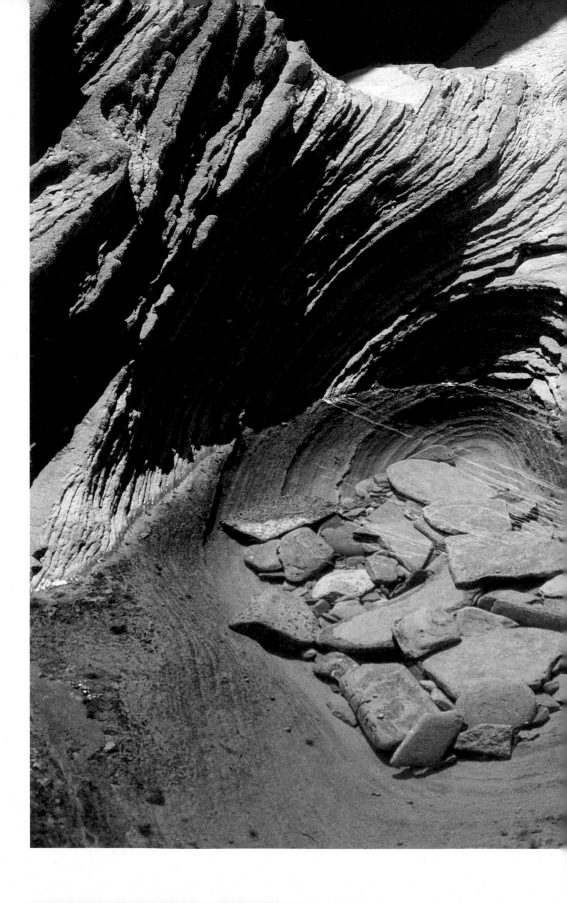

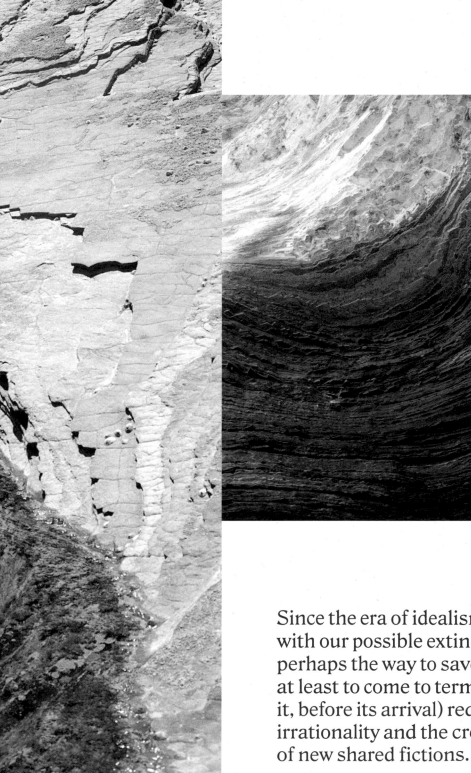

Since the era of idealism ends with our possible extinction, perhaps the way to save it (or at least to come to terms with it, before its arrival) requires irrationality and the creation of new shared fictions.

most responsible among the doomsayers are busy drafting up the
message to be left to any potential survivors —few in number and
primitive— lest they repeat our mistakes).

It's a recurring quote in opinion columns: Francis Fukuyama announced the end of history in 1992 after the dissolution of the USSR.
Today, however, while political history seems more alive than ever
(that illusion didn't last long — only until the 9/11 attacks), we have
come face to face with a new type of history, a natural history, that
once again presents us with the not so far-fetched possibility of our
disappearance as a species. This time, though, Khrushchev is not
there to negotiate on the other end of the red telephone.

So what then is this presence that threatens us? Or, to put it more
aggressively: where is the enemy?

THE IRRUPTION OF GAIA

In every text on the Anthropocene there is a section with this title. It
may be an "irruption" or an "interruption"; a "visit" that promises to
last forever; it may be "untimely", "inopportune" or "surprising"; in
any case, it seems that one fine day something pulled us out of our
collective reverie and began limiting our freedom and questioning
our privileges. Gaia forces us to rethink everything we've known.

Bruno Latour strongly believes that, eventually, the moment of dis-
covery by James Lovelock, a physiologist and engineer who studied
possible life on Mars in 1965, will become in the popular imagination
as clear and recognisable a scene as that of Galileo raising his tele-
scope towards the Moon from the Venetian Lagoon in 1609. If Galileo
discovered that all the stars resemble each other —thus expanding
the limits of knowledge from what his eye can see to the infinity of
the Universe—, Lovelock traced a symmetrical movement, albeit in
the opposite direction: he discovered the uniqueness of Earth (its
non-inert atmosphere), understanding it as a system in which geo-

chemical forces as well as all living organisms work in conjunction to keep the environment within the limits that are favourable for life.

Lovelock clarifies: "When I speak of Gaia as a superorganism, I'm not thinking of a goddess or a being endowed with thought. My intuition is that the Earth behaves in a self-regulating way and that the science best adapted to its study is physiology." Isabelle Stengers goes one step further and, although she begins by defining Gaia as "the dense set of relationships that connect what science used to treat separately, namely living beings, the atmosphere, the climate, the oceans...", a little later, in her book *In Catastrophic Times: Resisting the Coming Barbarism*, she goes on: "Gaia, the living planet, must be recognised as a being and not understood as merely a sum of processes, in the same sense in which we recognise that a mouse, for example, is a being. To interrogate Gaia is to interrogate a whole, and questions directed at a specific process can trigger an answer, perhaps unexpected, relating to the whole."

> We have discovered that we are fatally connected to everything that surrounds us.

The discomfort to which Gaia condemns us, Stengers continues, "constitutes an unprecedented, if not forgotten, form of transcendence: a fussy disposition of forces indifferent to our reasons and our designs."

It may not have been part of Lovelock's plans, but since Gaia is an unfathomable figure for modern science, one that undermines the power of humanity (we are, once again, dependent and vulnerable), she echoes so many traditions —not least her Greek goddess namesake— while also operating as suggestive metaphor: she has become a contemporary myth that fits perfectly with the definition given by cultural anthropologists.

More from Latour: "Gaia stands accused of being a religious idea disguised as science when, on the contrary, she forces us to reassess the knowledge learned from the past, including the strange notion that science should oppose religion. If we tried today, in the middle of the Anthropocene, to separate science and religion, we'd end up butch-

ering both due to the extent to which there is science contained in what we call religion and religion in what we understand as science."

In any case, since myth allows us to develop ideas, expectations and actions outside of logical rules, Gaia understood as myth —I'm now writing from a (suspiciously modern) place of pragmatism and necessity— could help us act to avoid being run over —paralysis, once again— by the "climate beast": believing in Gaia might save us from Gaia. This position, or something like it, is defended by philosopher and mathematician Jorge Riechmann, author of a vast body of work against the fetishisation of technology and in which he develops an "ethics of self-restraint," and recalls that *logos* (reason) always grow and take root in the mythical substrate.

But what if self-restraint is not enough? It's difficult to know where to turn to now that the walls of Modernity have collapsed, unable to contain the irruption of Gaia and her uncertainties. This isn't exactly a minor detail, not unlike the question of the Apocalypse, which had us convinced for years that it had already taken place (we had killed God) and that we were just splashing around in immobile time.

Brazilian anthropologist Eduardo Viveiros de Castro suggests asking indigenous peoples about the end of the world, since their world has been ending since 1500. Viveiros finds in the animist thought of the Amazonian peoples (broadly speaking, all things are permeated with humanity, thus there is no exceptionality in being human) an inclusive and trans-species way of negotiating with the environment. "What's important is to stop considering ourselves as a separate, privileged species that does not completely belong to the world, because it has an element that is outside of this world, a spiritual side, a cultural side, a linguistic side, symbolism, language, psychoanalysis. We contain something that separates us from reality and therefore we are complex, body and soul, while other entities only have bodies. If we attribute a 'soul' to everything, then everything is complex, just like us, or to put it another way, nothing is complex, therefore we're not complex."

If Gaia is a vengeful goddess (as has also been said about the coronavirus), we only have two options available to us: make our peace with her (we'd have a lot to learn from the Amerindian perspective),

"If we tried today, in the middle of the Anthropocene, to separate science and religion, we'd end up butchering both due to the extent to which there is science contained in what we call religion and religion in what we understand as science."
— Bruno Latour

or stand up and fight. Not to mention the fact that there is no enemy —not even Nature itself— capable of bringing all nations around the world to consensus, particularly considering that the interests of national governments are not even aligned with the needs of their own people or territory.

At this point, we are mired in helplessness and bewilderment. We have surrendered to the idea that the tools of Modernity —criticism and reason— are useless, and we have woven a quasi-religious narrative without even knowing if we're falling into naive shamanisms or unnecessary mysticisms. It seems all that's left to do is either pray to Gaia or indulge in cursed, thoughtless consumption à la Bataille.

Each author has a different view on the matter. The words of engineer and anthropologist Yayo Herrero seem —notice the adjective, I am once again dominated by the inertia of the Enlightenment— *reasonable*: "There is an ecological ceiling that we should not have broken through and a basic floor of needs, below which are lives that are not worth living. Between that basic floor and that ecological ceiling is a safe living space for humanity and for the rest of the living world that accompanies us on this planet."

And surely this will be, for the next few years —if we're still around, that is!— an exciting topic of debate, research and speculation. ▲

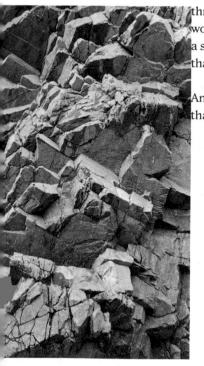

With computational power increasing exponentially and the metaverse just around the corner, the theory that we are living in a simulated reality is gaining ground. Its explanations of the meaning of life, a post-mortem existence and even a technological conception of God and Creation beg the question: could the simulation argument become the religion of the future?

LIFE IS A GAME

Text **Samuel Valiente** ▲ Illustrations **Ana Galvañ**

It happened a few months ago. One of the most anticipated —and later vilified— video games of recent years, Cyberpunk 2077, had just fallen into my hands and, despite not being much of a gamer, I *really* wanted a copy. So, after a long day of working from home, I decided to extend my stay in front of the computer for a few more hours... maybe six? Something like that, my memory is blurred. The fact is that, around 2am, I turned off the PC, got up from my chair, rubbed my eyes, went to the kitchen to get a glass of water, then to the bathroom to brush my teeth and, in each and every one of my movements, with each interaction —the dishes, the toothpaste, the mirror— I couldn't help feeling that my subjective experience was merely an extension of that first-person shooter marathon that I had just experienced. A feeling of unreality invaded me: I had the impression that, in a way, what we call real life was so similar to latest-generation video games —created, of course, in their image and likeness— that it would not be out of place to think that this could, in turn, have also been created as a simulation of another life, a more "real" life, which there would be no way of accessing because, after all, we would be nothing more than characters locked in a universe with specially elaborated physics and textures.

I didn't sleep well that night. I dreamed of a hodgepodge of laser guns and futuristic vehicles, and after that, I never played the damn video game again. That our existence is a simple simulation is an uncomfortable possibility. Uncomfortable, but no less likely. This idea has haunted our collective imagination, in a more or less primitive way, for centuries, but only in recent times have we begun to define it and take it seriously, by interacting directly with the technologies that could make it possible. Although it has recently had the semi-explicit endorsement of technological personalities such as Elon Musk or Ray Kurzweil, the first to raise this

possibility beyond a metaphysical joke was Nick Bostrom, a Swedish philosopher at the University of Oxford and an expert in transhumanism, AI and existential risk, who back in 2003 dared to pose the question in the form of an academic paper, that is, putting at risk his professional credibility: *Are You Living In A Computer Simulation?* His argument is actually very simple, and it could be summed up in the fact that at least one of these propositions is true: (1) the human species will become extinct before it reaches a post-human era; (2) a post-human civilisation would have no interest in generating simulated worlds; (3) we definitely live in a simulation. What's categorical about the third possibility is that, if a future civilisation were to create simulations (based or not on its own history), the number of simulations might be infinite (or, at least, it would be difficult to imagine there only being one), therefore the probability that we are living in the only non-simulated reality is negligible. I know: exploding head emoji.

Could we be facing a strangely plausible union between science and creationism, between the sacred and the pagan?

Of course, the idea that what we perceive as reality is nothing more than some kind of highly successful artifice is by no means a new one: it's been formulated in different ways throughout history, from Plato's Cave to the Cartesian hypothesis of the evil genius, the hyperreality and precession of Baudrillard's simulacra and Borges' relationship between maps and territories, or the life-as-a-dream literary trope that, even before

so ambitious that it transcends the borders of philosophy or science fiction, entering, or at least dipping its feet in, the even deeper waters of religion.

And this is where the theory gets particularly interesting. Because, if we assume that we live in a simulation, we accept to a greater or lesser extent that there is a creative entity or entities, that life has a certain purpose, that there is one or more higher planes of existence (which we may eventually access at the end of our "lives") and that we are being watched by an omnipresent being or beings (who

There are those who believe that all consciences are copies of each other and that when we "die" we reincarnate in another simulated body.

Calderón de la Barca, was constantly cropping up across the most distant cultures and civilisations. However, there's a difference between all these hypotheses, approaches, myths or stories and the simulation argument: unlike the former, which offer a symbolic approach or try to explain a sociological phenomenon, the latter presents itself as a possible scientific explanation for existence in its entirety. Philosopher David Pearce —and Bostrom's transhumanist colleague— called the simulation argument "perhaps the first interesting explanation of the existence of a Creator in 2000 years." An assertion that, although it requires much diluting considering the friendship between both thinkers, doesn't seem negligible to me. Regardless of the effective feasibility of the theory – which, with respect to my limitations, I will not expand on — we are facing an explanation

might also be judging us). In other words: the simulation argument could corroborate, through science, what the vast majority of religions have been proposing throughout history. Could we be facing a strangely plausible union between science and creationism, between the sacred and the pagan?

Of course, the simulation theory is currently a tremendously risky one (to begin with, the computing power to generate a work of such magnitude is unthinkable for now), but the seed of credibility that technology brings with it, added to the blind faith that we already profess to it and the acceleration of its progress, make it a potential candidate to become, one day, a more or less acceptable credo. Let's think about this: would a member of Generation Z or later, born firmly into digital technology, be more likely to believe in angels and miracles, or in almighty computers? Not surprisingly, references to the subject on social media and in popular culture are on the up: articles about it proliferate, expressions such as "the simulation is broken" or "glitch in the Matrix" are increasingly common (despite the 22 years since the release of the well-known film) and series like *Rick & Morty* or *The Midnight Gospel* constantly explore the issue. One particular episode of the latter series launched a brilliant reflection on spirituality, reducing it to absurdity using —more or less metaphorically— the simulation theory: "Let's think of any spiritual practice that tries to achieve an objective, like 'I'm going to be more spiritual,' 'I'm going to be more loving' [...] Man, you're a slave in World of Warcraft. Step away from the fucking computer. Wake up! It's just a game. You work non-stop in World of Warcraft. You engage in spiritual practices, trying to gain experience points with a character that doesn't even exist. You've lost sight of the fact that it's all just a game. Man, you're dehydrated, drink some water. You've been playing non-stop for 20 hours, you've forgotten you were playing a game." A devastating vision, but also strangely liberating, in its own way.

BELIEVERS AND FANATICS

Beyond the clickbait headlines, memes and more or less profound fictions, however, there are more and more people who take the subject seriously. Some of them take it *very* seriously indeed. We might even call them believers. Convinced disciples who elaborate their own theories, branching off from the main hypothesis, generally evading any scientific argument. Thus, there are those who believe that all consciences are copies of each other and that when we "die" we reincarnate in another simulated body, or that the meaning of life is to repeat it over and over again to obtain knowledge (something like experience points) un-

Would a member of Generation Z or later, born firmly into digital technology, be more likely to believe in angels and miracles, or in almighty computers?

til we finally leave the simulation and, somehow, "win the game." The various contributions that one finds on the web, to be honest, seem to be nothing more than instances. There are even gurus on the subject, of course, like Thomas W. Campbell. Author of *My Big TOE: Awakening: A Trilogy Unifying Philosophy, Physics, and Metaphysics* (TOE is short for Theory Of Everything), Campbell relies on the simulation hypothesis (which, unlike Bostrom, he takes for granted with complete certainty) to provide a sort of "guide for life" with the classic New Age combination of quantum mechanics, law of attraction and psychomagic (shaken, not stirred).

Faith in God, in reincarnation, in spirits or in a divine computer of the future, what difference does it make? Faith is faith.

At this point, and as is usual in human nature (especially in relation to beliefs and religions), its inevitable dark and dangerous side begins to emerge. The oldest and most popular subreddit on the subject, r/SimulationTheory, had to be shut down by its own creator last year after a decade of activity. The reason was explained by the admin himself: "This subreddit has turned into an amplification machine for the paranoid thoughts of troubled minds. I cannot in good conscience keep this sub active, it is outright immoral." Apparently, some of its members were taking the theory too far: there were those who believed

themselves to be the only "real" consciousness and that they were surrounded by NPCs (in video games, non-playable characters), a term that has also been used in political memes —frequently of far-right tendency— to refer to empty or "soulless" individuals. Others threatened to commit suicide to break the simulation. There were also persecutory delusions like *The Truman Show*, and there were even those who claimed to hear the voices of the "Creator." Could a Church of Simulation ever be created? If so, and looking back at human history, its fundamentalists would soon be with us too.

Feeling uneasy after browsing Reddit, I decide to ask a question to my contacts through Instagram Stories. What does my social circle think about this theory? Would they change their way of life if they knew that their very existence is a simulation? Surprisingly, the answer that I encountered again and again is, "I wouldn't change anything." @dr.berni responds: "If you believe in the existence of an afterlife, you're already living as if an afterlife existed." And he's right: simulation theory is, today —and always will be— unprovable, so we can only relate to it in the same way that we relate to religion: through faith alone. So that "theory of everything" is still, for practical purposes, a theory of nothing. Faith in God, in reincarnation, in spirits or in a divine computer of the future, what difference does it make? Faith is faith. You can take it more or less seriously and try to tear the tissues of reality to unmask the simulation, or you can take it as a great cosmic joke, in the style of *The Midnight Gospel*, and simply focus on enjoying life, simulated or not. At the end of the day, as @areicuts said in his Stories: "Wine is cool just the same." ▲

Text Alejandro Zambudio ▲ Images Irene Molina

7.000 MILLION PROPHETS

How liberalism and postmodernism commodify faith and sacralise identity.

The question of identity has polarised history and public opinion for centuries. Faith in religion used to help us define a communal identity. Europe was born as a common identity: especially in the times of the Crusades, and in the 16th and 17th centuries. The Europe of the Treaty of Maastricht and Lisbon was not only a union between peoples: it was also a religious union. Today, however, these ideas have lost relevance and we find ourselves at a time in history in which identities, detached in this case from the dogma of the Catholic Church, have become one of the highest aspirations of the liberal system. An aspiration that, enhanced by social networks, has proliferated countless new identities alien to the great discourses of religion.

The West exchanged its religious identity for social identity. The process was complex, but the institutions changed and civil power rose over religious power. As civil power grew, its citizens were gradually gaining more and more interest in politics. Alexis de Tocqueville, in *Democracy in America*, recounted this change: European society had already reached a degree of complexity in which, to avoid revolts, kings and nobles had to create interest groups among citizens for them to compete peacefully with each other. Western secularisation began around 200 years

ago. Before that, religion played a central role, when knowledge, an almost exclusive property of the Church, served to provide answers to the mystery of the human soul. In the modern world, however, the development of more complex institutions, as well as the rise of scientific thought, eventually turned the tables around.

During the lives of our parents and grandparents, community ties were strengthened in churches and other rites of worship. Society was much more closed and the presence of religion in our lives kept us safe from others and from ourselves. As globalisation progressed, the new world order led by the United States seized political and cultural hegemony, entrusting us to the market as a god figure. It is in this phase of propaganda and absorption of other cultures that identity becomes commercialised. The postmodern paradigm reaches its peak, renewing, for better or for worse, our way of understanding identity issues. Postmodernity seduced us with its mixture of elements, styles, and eras; it did away with the distinctions between high and low culture thanks to the sublimation of the mass and the popular, the ancient and the modern. We build our current identity on the basis of the historical, cultural and political present, without preambles and solemnity, while religious identity gave more importance to ritual and social hierarchies. The liberal system sheltered us with its promises of prosperity: now it is the market, and not God, who is in charge of shaping the individual and collective aspirations of the human being.

Science and technology also displaced religion in the twentieth century: exploring the infinitely large and infinitely small, reshaping life, offering a semblance of immortality. Biomedicine and biotechnology advanced. The quality of life improved. And, in parallel, Western society turned to hedonism and narcissism. Something that the rise of social networks only accelerated, turning the cult of the body and oneself into a true religion. If modern society believed in the future, universality, revolution and reason at the

The modern era was obsessed with production and revolution, the postmodern era is obsessed with information and expression.

collective level, today we find a society that seeks more individual well-being than great political projects. There is no longer a linear narrative of events and thanks to the internet, new voices have proliferated and multiplied. Gilles Lipovetsky explains it perfectly in *Hypermodern Times*: "Once the past and the future have been discredited, there is a tendency to think that the present is the essential reference for democratic individuals, since they have definitively broken with the traditions that modernity has swept away, and they have returned from those tomorrows that they hardly had a chance to praise."

In today's society, the analysis of this phenomenon is better explained through seduction than by ideas such as alienation or discipline. We no longer have prescribed models for social groups, but behaviours chosen and assumed by individuals; nor norms imposed without discussion, but a will to seduce that affects the public domain indistinctly. The modern era was obsessed with production and revolution, the postmodern era is obsessed with information and expression.

In this self-asserting narrative, economic liberalism, through the market and through advertising, sells the individual the possibility of prospering thanks to the cult of the self. Perhaps that is why the system is interested in how our identity is subject to economic performance: today seduction is much stronger than coercive power. We need to share freely, disclose every detail of ourselves. Hence, large companies market t-shirts with feminist slogans or initiatives such as the green economy emerge. It must be made clear that, by freely sharing our adherence to a certain group, we are better people. More virtuous. Capitalism always finds new identities to exploit. It feeds on the struggle and oppression of the rest, co-opting their slogans and demands. It manages to empty the ideological content of all identities to subject them to the scrutiny of the market.

We cooperate, often actively, in this process. In the coaching society, humans have become entrepreneurs of themselves, their own personal brand. We find that personal brand in the exaltation of our identity. Byung-Chul Han considers that in "the exposed society, each subject is their own publicity object. Everything is measured in its exposure value. The exposed society is a pornographic society". Therefore, many people are not as interested in following a certain belief as they are in ensuring that others know that they are following it. Thus, in the meetings of these individuals (united, in this case, as a collective) we witness the new endogamous repetition of a

We witness the new endogamous repetition of a rite whose object is the group's own predilection for itself.

rite whose object is the group's own predilection for itself. And, similarly, for the hatred of the adversary. Samuel P. Huntington, in his book *Clash of Civilizations*, wrote that "hatred defines any type of political and social structure. Unless we hate something or someone, we can never define an identity." Social networks, led by Twitter, are only proof of this.

Current historical projects and the social field represent the extension of the private sphere. If we say in a conversation that we are vegan or that we defend the rights of trans people, to give two examples, we discover that it's not enough simply to position ourselves in favour: we must also express our hatred towards bullfighters or the "mansplainers" who write *El País*. And, in the same vein, a true "patriot" will not be considered by their people as such unless they continually show their merciless rejection towards any element considered by the group as an "enemy" of its particular idea of homeland. This happens because consensus is not only generated through union: opposition to specific values or animosity towards a common adversary are the best catalysts for the emergence of an identity. And, in this sense, the media play a major role as it prioritises identities and discourses related to these issues. The media, like the Church in ages past, is the institution that ultimately determines what is good and what is bad.

These are not good times for criticism and debate. In identity groups, what Sloterdijk, in *Critique of Cynical Reason*, calls "enlightened false consciousness" often occurs. He and other rationalists of his time miss knowledge, argumentation, the middle grounds used in reasoning and debate, as was the case in the times of the Enlightenment and modernism. With postmodernity, on the contrary, emotion is exalted over

reason. We see this in many identity groups, who sometimes prefer to speak in terms of "historical grievances" rather than the present. In identity groups and in contemporary society, we attach more importance to personal or culturally specific facts and the privilege of "lived experience"

Opposition to specific values or animosity towards a common adversary are the best catalysts for the emergence of an identity.

over empirical evidence. As Helen Pluckrose aptly emphasises in *How French "Intellectuals" Ruined the West: Postmodernism and Its Impact*, "relativistic ideas, sensitivity to language, and focus on identity over humanity or individuality have become dominant in society in general. It is much easier to say what one feels than to rigorously examine the evidence. The freedom to 'interpret' reality according to the values of each person is fed by the very human tendency to resort the confirmation bias and motivated reasoning."

Cristopher Butler, correctly, declares that "the individual, with their characteristics, their identity, in their connection with themselves, is the product of a power relation that is exerted on bodies, multiplicities, movements, desires, forces," and states that "there is almost no room left for individuality or autonomy." By excluding the individual from being considered as such within a group, in favour of the so-called "group identity," there is sometimes the effect that the subject himself, who adheres to the group to claim its essence, sees how this is put aside for the sake of the survival of the group in which it is found. It is, perhaps, the only aspect in which the identities of the postmodern era and religion converge: the punishment of anyone who deviates from the orthodoxy of the group and tries to put their interests above the collective.

And, despite the above, despite the great complexity of today's societies, we continue to need identities. And we need them because human beings, today reduced to their role as producer-consumers in an increasingly mechanised society, need to be part of something, even if it's through social networks. The asepsis of everyday life has robbed us of our sense of belonging. Nietzschian and Heideggerian nihilism has shaped a society that tries to flee from its burdens, assimilating identities constructed through a medium as artificial as the internet. We are part of a wheel that doesn't stop turning and that is distorting, precisely, what it seems to defend so vigorously: the identity of the individual. ▲

NO EVI- DENCE BUT

Text Natalia Carranza ▲ Images David Dees

NO DOUBT

Born out of healthy suspicion, but fuelled by the excesses of social media and the increasing complexity of the world, conspiracies jump from smartphone to smartphone and from mind to mind at pandemic speed. What's behind this kind of negative faith?

Few people know the true origin of the cherry tomato, that variety that in the late nineties invaded our salads seemingly out of nowhere. In 1974, the United States Army sought synergies with the food industry to test a series of genetic procedures that would allow the maximum concentration of plant and vegetable nutrients in order to minimise transportation and storage costs. The pilot test was a success, but it had a trade-off: Monsanto, the company they collaborated with, required the introduction of their proprietary fungicide into the process. A fungicide that, as is known today, causes cancer in high doses. But what seemed like a problem turned into an advantage, as the pharmaceutical industry also invested in the project for its potential economic benefits. A win for everyone... except the consumer.

This fact has not transpired, of course, because the powerful don't want it to be known. Or... because I just made it up. But you can't deny that cherry tomatoes are strange enough to arouse suspicion. It's normal: suspicion is a defence mechanism to protect ourselves from others and to anticipate their evil intentions, as explained by professor of social and organisational psychology Jan-Willem van Prooijen in his article *Suspicion Makes us Human*. Furthermore, evolutionary theories suggest that, when the cost of a false positive —considering something to be a threat without it being a threat— is different from the cost of a false negative —not considering something to be a threat when it is in fact a threat— the natural selection benefits the error that has a lower cost. And this is usually the false positive. That is to say: if my story were true and the cherry tomato were really carcinogenic, ignoring it would carry a very high cost, so we will instinctively tend to believe it.

Suspicion is indeed instinctive, but sometimes we try to rationalise it to convince others (or even ourselves) despite not having much to grasp beyond our own intuition. This is when the attempt to explain the suspicion can go wrong. Noel Ceballos, journalist and author of *The Conspiracy Thought* (2021), compares it to that episode of *The Simpsons* in which the children of Springfield believe that their fathers and mothers have become daytime vampires, when in reality what's happening is that, powered by a stimulating tonic that everyone has bought, they lock themselves in their rooms before dark to have sex. They perceive something strange; they fear that something bad is happening and they struggle to find

an explanation, but "due to lack of experience, they still cannot interpret the facts correctly."

FROM SUSPICION TO CONSPIRACY

Conspiracy theories emerge from a mixture of suspicion, the attempt to make sense of it and the inability to understand certain situations, a negative faith that rejects official sources and clings to parallel discourses. These, explains researcher Karen Douglas in *Understanding Conspiracy Theories*, deal with the causes and circumstances of social or political events on topics as broad and diverse as science, health, the environment, immigration, racism, terrorism or the international relations, affirming the existence of secret plots conducted by powerful actors. There may be lone wolves who plan to harm us, but one person alone does not conspire, he always

needs others. Thus, these theories are supported by *others* with the intention of harming *us*.

If suspicion is innate to humans, conspiracy theories must be as old as *Homo sapiens* himself. *Suspicion Makes Us Human* gathers together some historical examples: from the Greek myth in which the women of Lemnos unite to kill their husbands after discovering that they have been deceived, to the medieval stories that claimed that the Jews murdered each year a child to use his blood in religious rituals. According to Ceballos, each era gathers its fears and anxieties in conspiracy theories, and if before they were personified in women, Jews, Freemasons and Communists, today the *others* are doctors, scientists, pharmaceutical companies, governments and rich government officials. Thus, some of the current theories affirm that the attack on the Twin Towers was a false flag attack, that Trump is saving the world from a network of cannibalistic paedophiles, among which are Hillary Clinton, Barack Obama and Tom Hanks, or that the coronavirus is an excuse to inject ourselves with a Microsoft chip.

It may sound like crazy, but it would be wrong to dismiss the scope and popularity of these theories. According to a study published in The Harvard Kennedy School, in March 2020, when the health crisis had just erupted in Europe, one in three Americans believed in some conspiracy theory. His suspicions, moreover, are not entirely unfounded: we have seen how institutions that ensure our safety and well-being have used people as guinea pigs. A good example is Project MK-Ultra, in which the CIA and 80 other institutions, including universities, hospitals,

Suspicion is a defence mechanism
to protect ourselves from others
and to anticipate their evil intentions.

prisons, and pharmaceutical companies, tried to develop substances that would facilitate mind control by experimenting with US citizens, administering LSD and other chemicals without their consent. Several deaths have been associated with the project, but since the program was secret and illegal, its full scope will never be known. The truth is that cases of abuse of power between governments, powerful individuals and billionaires, capable of doing and undoing with impunity, are not uncommon. Take, for example, Epstein, an alleged friend of both Trump and Clinton, among many others, who abused minors and prostituted them with privileged men whom he recorded to obtain material with which to blackmail them. Is it crazy to suspect that he might not commit suicide in his cell?

It's to be expected that, with cases like these, we not only suspect the official sources, but many are willing to embrace as dogma everything that goes against it. In 2018, only 37% of people said they trusted medicine, up from more than 60% half a century ago. The same thing happens in the political arena: until the 1960s, the faith of the American population in their government exceeded 50%; from that moment on, it begins to decline and falls to 17% in 2019, according to the Pew Research Center. And it was not only the Trump factor that had an influence, since Obama's maximum was 26% (curious fact: G. W. Bush managed to reach 54%, to later blow up that trust again with non-existent weapons of mass destruction). Thomas Milan Konda, author of the book *Conspiracies of Conspiracies*, calls this historical period "the end of trust."

Another key ingredient in the spread of conspiracy theories has been, of course, the internet. The proliferation of discordant discourses has always coincided with the population's access to new means of communication, according to Jaume Aguilar, Communications Professor at the University of Barcelona: "A revolution as exceptional as the internet, or as the printing press was in its time, causes a paradigm shift in the transmission of knowledge and the subsequent debate on form, content and the criteria behind the definition of 'truth' or 'lies'. At the same time, actors appear who want their economic and political control. This is why today we see an increase in populist and authoritarian tendencies. Just as writing expanded the 'spectacular' function of the word and the printing press, today we are experiencing another moment of 'spectacularisation'."

Social media has also connected more than half of the world's population and given us the power to publish and broadcast what we want, when we want it. "Hoaxes and fake news travel faster and faster and denials come later," says Noel Ceballos. "At the beginning of the 20th century, if you wanted to make a libel like *The Protocols of the Elders of Zion*, you had to go from country to country finding a printer who wanted to get it out and you had to distribute a few copies that circulated from hand to hand. Now, with Telegram and WhatsApp that process is instantaneous and you reach the entire world at once."

CONSPIRACY AS A PANDEMIC

The actors and the media were on standby. The only thing missing was a disruptive event, of which we had no experience and that affected all of us, to definitively make conspiracy theories go mainstream. And it came in the form of a virus. "The pandemic has acted like napalm on conspiracy thinking," says the journalist. "When I started writing the book in 2019, it was something that was on the margins of discourse. Now

The truth is that cases of abuse of power between governments, powerful individuals and billionaires, capable of doing and undoing with impunity, are not uncommon.

it's come to the centre. The pandemic has been a brutal paradigm shift, and the changes cause vertigo and mistrust about the future." But, as he adds, the change is abstract and our fear of it is hard to explain. Instead, conspiracy theories help give you specific names and surnames.

Fear does not understand left or right. Although we tend to associate conspiracy thinking with the more conservative positions, there is no shortage of conspiracy and populist theories on the other side. Miguel Bosé, who supported Zapatero (Spanish former socialist president) a few years ago, now shares videos on social media in which he says that behind the coronavirus vaccines there is "a cartel of psychopathic billionaires called the Davos Forum." In fact, the anti-vaccine movement has traditionally been associated with the mainstream of spirituality and the New Age. Based on an eclectic mix of Western and Eastern doctrines, this movement believes that we are about to make an evolutionary leap in the level of human consciousness, that we have innate spiritual capacities that have effects on the health of our body, mind and soul, and that the truth must be experienced person-

ally, without allowing itself to be contaminated by social conventions.

This group has been one of the most permeable to conspiracy theories in recent years. So much so that there is even a name for the phenomenon: Conspirituality. The first academic reference to this term is from 2011, proposed by anthropologists Charlotte Ward and David Voas. According to their work, conspiracy thinking puts on the table a problem for which the evolutionary leap of the New Agers has a solution: it's only necessary to activate the new paradigm with the awakening of conscience to fight against the imposed political and social order by a group that tries to control us.

To a significant extent, the pandemic has also accelerated the convergence between conspiracists and spiritualists because the latter have had to move their meeting spaces from the physical world —more closed and limited— to the digital environment —more open and, therefore, more susceptible to mixing with others. Shortly after the lockdown, denialist messages began to spread on their platforms, causing some of their

Just as writing expanded the 'spectacular' function of the word and the printing press, today we are experiencing another moment of 'spectacularisation'.

members to be alerted. Azadeh Ghafari, a psychotherapist who manages @the.wellness.therapist Instagram account, explained in the Mother Jones media how users she follows began to share crazy theories. Yoga teacher Seane Corn, who admits to being critical of modern medicine, told the BBC that during the pandemic she would have received messages to participate in anti-vaccine panels that denied the existence of the coronavirus. And Matthew Remski, writer and consultant for yoga and Ayurveda, examines the toxic ties between conspiracy and the New Age in a podcast called Conspirituality, no less.

The connection process between the two, however, is not as naive as it seems. A study by the Center for Countering Digital Hate (CCDH) revealed that anti-vaccine influencers, including those who are part of the New Age community, have gained eight million followers since 2019. In total, we speak of 31 million people following these accounts in Facebook groups and another 17 million subscribed to similar accounts on YouTube. As Remski says, with yoga studios closed during confinement, some influencers in the discipline have found an opportunity to stand

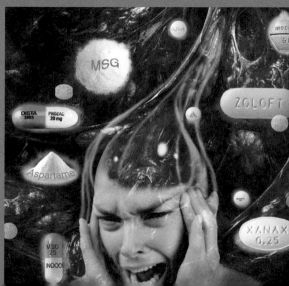

There are YouTube channels offering their faithful an almost uninterrupted flow of unfiltered conspiracy information. And they are monetising these videos.

out on social media by posting fake news, which, according to a study by DAS Insurance, has up to 70% more possibilities of being shared than the real ones.

And in the meantime, what are Big Tech doing to curb conspiracy? Not much, apparently. We should not be surprised, taking into account that they also get their share: "There are YouTube channels [...] offering their faithful an almost uninterrupted flow of unfiltered conspiracy information. And they are monetising these videos, of course," says Ceballos. In fact, the CCDH estimates that advertising revenue from conspiratorial messages amounts to one trillion dollars annually. The Amazon paradox is also curious: although Jeff Bezos, CEO of the company until very recently, was a constant target of conspiracists, the platform shamelessly sells flat-earth, anti-vaccine and climate change denier books.

Instead, Facebook announced in 2020 that it would remove all accounts and pages linked to QAnon, one of the most popular conspiracy theories, from its platforms. Beyond the doubts that the criteria of a company like this may arouse to decide what is true and what is a lie, what is be-

ing proven is the ineffectiveness of its validation systems. Since the deletion of accounts began, the ones who have suffered are the users, the only thing shared by them with the conspirators is the use of words that they have appropriated. In addition, there are those who consider that this policy not only does misses the root problem, but it doesn't even mitigate it. According to a study by researchers Justin E. Lane, Kevin McCaffree and F. LeRon Shults, banning users can incentivise them to search for other online spaces where they connect with people with the same beliefs. Much like a sect, the isolation to which they are condemned ends up making their negative faith more radical and shielding themselves from events outside their bubble.

So what can be done to curb conspiracy thinking? Ceballos proposes two remedies. On the one hand, not trying to impose a vision, but fighting conspiratorial dogma with questions that encourage debate and critical thinking. And, on the other hand, counteracting the suspicion with Ockham's razor to apply the simplest explanation. But in an environment that will surely be the victim of new health, social or environmental crises, where knowledge is atomised, the lie trav-

els through the same channels and at the same
—or faster— speed than the truth and technological development takes more and more speed,
simple explanations are going to be fewer and
far between. Are we, therefore, doomed to conspiracy thinking? "Maybe so," replies Ceballos.
"It won't go away; it will be maintained and who
knows if it'll keep growing."

Van Prooijen believes that we have changed the
world at a rate with which our brain, tied to the
tempo of biological evolution, cannot catch up.
In this new context, suspicion, which until now
had helped us survive, becomes dysfunctional
and can work against us. And faced with this, we
are left with two options: find a way to get rid of
that instinct or slow down the pace of progress
(somewhat unlikely) so as not to continue wid-
ening the gap. Although this, of course, is only
a theory. And, if I lied to you about the cherry
tomatoes, who can assure you that I haven't done
it again? ▲

David Dees has arguably been the most prominent artist dedicated to conspiracy theories. He began as an illustrator on Sesame Street but his career was cut short by a growing disenchantment with paranoid overtones that led him to dedicate his life to illustrating conspiracy theories. David Dees died of cancer in May 2020 at the age of 62. All the images, in the public domain, have been transferred to 'La nueva carne' by filmmaker Brad Abrahams, author of the documentary about the artist's life, 'Do you see what I see?'

THE MAGI- CAL SCI- ENCE OF QUAN- TUM MYSTI- CISM

Illustrations
Marina Colell
@graphitons

Text
Adriana Royo

Science against religion, physics against spirituality, reason against faith. We have seen how religion has condemned and persecuted science, or how science has opposed scripture. Sceptics who underestimate dogma, scientists who deny God, religious orthodox disciples against atheistic rationalists. Some believers have attacked scientific contributions and, in parallel, scientists have attacked the theological perspective on many occasions in an illegitimate and cruel way. Today, science and technology have superseded faith. There are more than 3,000 years of mystical thinking on our planet, but it seems that now this tradition needs a more empirical legitimacy. Has science finally superseded faith? Do we have faith in science? Do we still have faith in anything at all?

Humans continue to ask themselves the same fundamental questions: where we come from, why we are here, what God, the spirit, causality and the afterlife are or what they *could* be, what the origin of thought and the nature of consciousness are. Physics studies the fundamental rules with which the world works: it is intellectual, conscious work, which requires logic and reason, while mysticism deals with experience itself, with subjectivity, the intimate. Can scientists explain what consciousness is without philosophising? Can mystics corroborate their illuminations? Does physics have something to say about the spirit? Is love measurable? Who are the holders of the truth: those who manage to verify their hypotheses? Those who believe without the need for evidence? We long to establish a faith, a theory capable of explaining everything, to decipher the unknown, to be right and to settle within safe limits, without the horrifying abyss of chaos. We long to avoid that existential orphanhood, that anguish. What is the universe if not deep and impenetrable in its infinite mystery? We long to tear at the veils of the universe to comprehend it. Do we need wars for that?

One of the current ideas that has been the object of controversy —as well as celebration— is quantum mysticism: a mystical belief with pseudoscientific overtones and Eastern mystical convictions. A bridge between the most scientific to the most spiritual, with an increasing number of supporters. Let's take a step back: classical physics —Newtonian physics— is objective and describes the movement of particles and objects according to deterministic laws, so future events can be predicted through the observation of everyday events. If I push someone off a roof, gravity will pull them to the ground, causing certain death. But at the beginning of the 20th century, a group of scientists discovered a new way of perceiving reality: the functioning of subatomic matter —atoms and particles at the microcosmic level—, waves and particles that behave differently when observed, that is to say, they do not exist as such, but are a trend expressed in terms of probabilities. Pure speculation.

The problem with quantum physics is that it does not predict specific events, but only probabilities that change according to the observer, and this cannot be studied by physics, since it adds a subjective part to the equation. Some scientists, like Niels Bohr, considered that the consciousness of the observer was what modified the observed. Others, like Einstein, believed that a simple thermometer could contribute to this phenomenon. It was in 1927 that the scientific community also became divided, with Einstein accusing Bohr of committing the mistake of combining science with mysticism.

Science borders on philosophical aspects, but it cannot corroborate them. Mysticism, being a subjective experience, cannot corroborate them either, but is there something that unites them? Doesn't science also require faith?

Those who decided to believe that the power of consciousness generated one reality or another laid the foundations of the New Age, and during the seventies books such as *The Tao of Physics* by physicist Fritjof Capra, or *Dancing Wu li Masters* by Gary Zukav were written, connecting, among other things, Buddhism and physics. During

The New Age spiritualists took the premises of quantum physics one by one and imported them to spirituality.

the 2000s, best sellers emerged that endowed transcendent phenomena with science, such as *The Power of Now*, *The Secret* or the well-known documentary *What the Bleep Do We Know!?*, offering voice and faith to a new generation of people who were already a bit restless, or weren't satisfied with the idea of the human body as a simple machine, or the concept of religion as an authority to obey in order to be rewarded at the end of life. The New Age spiritualists took the premises of quantum physics one by one and imported them to spirituality: the subatomic atoms represented the micro of a higher fractal of the spirit. As subatomic phenomena do not give certainties and the only thing we can do is predict their probabilities, we influence our reality. As any object has the ability to be in several positions at the same time (Einstein called it "spooky action at a distance"), we create our reality. Since two particles are intertwined and affect each other, you and I are the

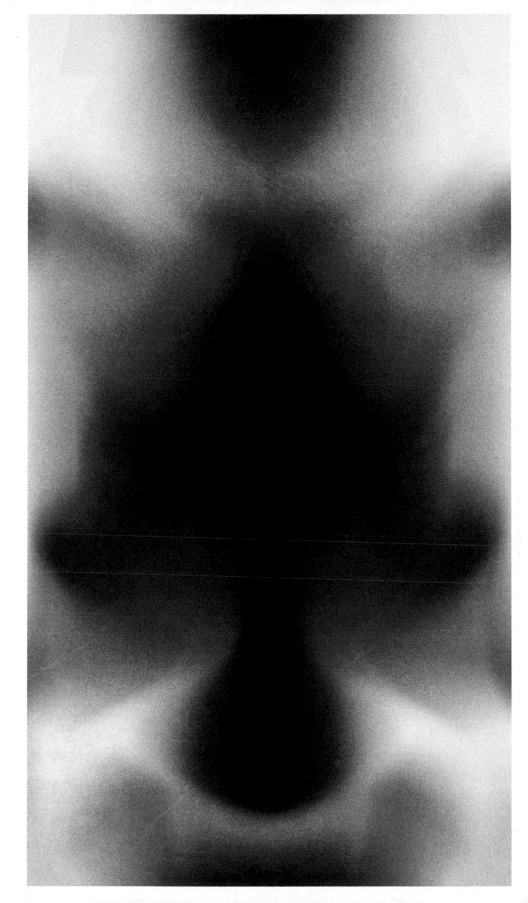

same, and if I hurt myself, I hurt you. The power of your thought affects your reality, you influence the world and nothing happens by chance. Was it a smart, generous way to link the two ideas, or simply a commercial gold mine?

As in any field, this New Age also saw the rise of New Scammers, who took the opportunity to steal concepts from quantum physics to better market their courses, in an atomic hodgepodge easily saleable to the undecided, the lazy and the lost, discrediting both science and mysticism in the process. This belief has branched out and taken root not only in the form of faith but as a fashion that has conquered the health market as miracle therapies that claim to cure depression, anxiety disorders, chronic pain or even cancer. Quantum energy therapies, quantum medicine, quantum diets, sacred geometry. Heal your discomfort by balancing your cellular vibration! Anyone can become an expert by reading *The Secret*, regurgitating information without any criticism or reflection and offering workshops to anyone who is nervous enough to go looking for some kind of answer to calm their existential anxiety.

But, beyond scammers and phonies, which can be found anywhere, thanks to the technological and mental advancement resulting from opening ourselves up to the possibilities of combining science and faith, several scientists have taken things one step further with experiments in which the subjective and the objective have joined forces for a greater good. In recent years there have been several experiments on the power of the mind through meditation and its effectiveness on stress, anxiety, depression, aging or diseases such as Alzheimer's. This can be proven by studying by computed tomography that occurs in the brain during meditation. One of the latest studies led by Clifford Saron at the University of California

shows changes in more than twenty genes after three weeks on a meditation retreat. There is also a famous trial in Washington, D.C. conducted by John Hagelin, a doctor in physics from Harvard University, between 2007 and 2010, in which a group of 2,500 people with experience in meditation managed to reduce acts of violence in the city, in particular the rate of homicide and violent crime. The intention and attention of all those

There have been several experiments on the power of the mind through meditation and its effectiveness on stress, anxiety, depression, aging or diseases such as Alzheimer's.

meditating people had an impact on subsequent social dynamics: violence fell by 21.2% and it is estimated that about 8,157 homicides were prevented.

During the 1990s, physicist Anton Zeilinger explained to the Dalai Lama that when one investigates the nature of an electron, one doesn't actually find it because it is empty, and that it only exists in relation to the observer. The Dalai Lama replied that, for Buddhism, the self as such does not exist, as it is constantly changing, and that when one enters deep concentration through meditation —a contemplative method of investigating the mind— one disappears. There is neither the observed nor the observer, nor is there any observation itself. Both agreed that nothing exists independently and everything is inter-related.

The two hemispheres of the brain come to mind, their way of elaborating and processing information. Each one sees the world differently: the left part perceives it logically, linearly, rationally, and it is attributed to analysis, mathematics or writing, while the right part integrates emotions, sensations, smells, images or sounds, and it is attributed to our perception of the world. The two sides are not in contact with one another, but a structure formed by millions of nerve fibres called

The mystical tradition enters into dialogue with the neurosciences: mind and body, right and left, science and spirituality united not to conquer, but to learn.

the *corpus callosum* connects them coordinating the functions of both. Its function is to serve as a system of communication for the two to work in a complementary way. Each one takes care of itself, one is not better than the other and, it goes without saying, one does not have greater access to the truth than the other.

We all have two hemispheres, but our tendency is to feel more comfortable when using one of them. People more inclined to the left hemisphere live their life from this more logical and "precise" perspective. They have more rational characters, they like to study, argue, verify, and need to feel that they control a situation when making decisions. They tend to be rigid and have a hard time letting go, they are guided more by the "should" of life and have strong morale. They have a tough time being in touch with their emotions and they don't trust unconscious processes as much. People more inclined towards their right hemisphere, on the other hand, have a more emotional mentality, are more sensitive, perceptive and intuitive, and need to express themselves from a more ar-

tistic and irrational side. They feel safe acting according to how they feel, without analysing it too much. They both feel and think, but they organise their lives from different perspectives. If, for example, we took a more rational person and a more artistic one, it would not be difficult for either of them to understand how the other perceives reality. However, I see around me a great communication problem between these two ways of conceiving life.

Knowledge of science reflects a conscious, objective and solid reality, but reality is also subjective, unconscious and ambiguous. It is difficult for us to contain that duality and live with it. We live in permanent conflict, without reaching an agreement, such as when we desire someone who does not suit us and our logic dictates that we move on, but our passion wants us to stick around, or when we want to leave a job that doesn't satisfy us but we hold on, despite our anxiety, because common sense warns us that we won't make ends meet.

I'm neither a scientist or a mystic, but through my experience as a therapist I have observed a large number of patients with complex and deep-rooted conflicts that I still cannot say how they have resolved. On one occasion, a thirty-four-year-old patient came in exhausted after three years trying to have a child with her partner. Both, healthy and fertile, were about to start IVF treatment. She came to me to manage the stress, fears and relationship problems that the situation caused her. She wondered if she would be a good mother, if she would end up neglecting her child, if her partner would leave her. She believed that she would not have children because of a divine punishment, she felt low and sometimes fell into periods of depression. During our conversations something caught my attention, so I decided to pull on the thread. In two sessions we looked into her

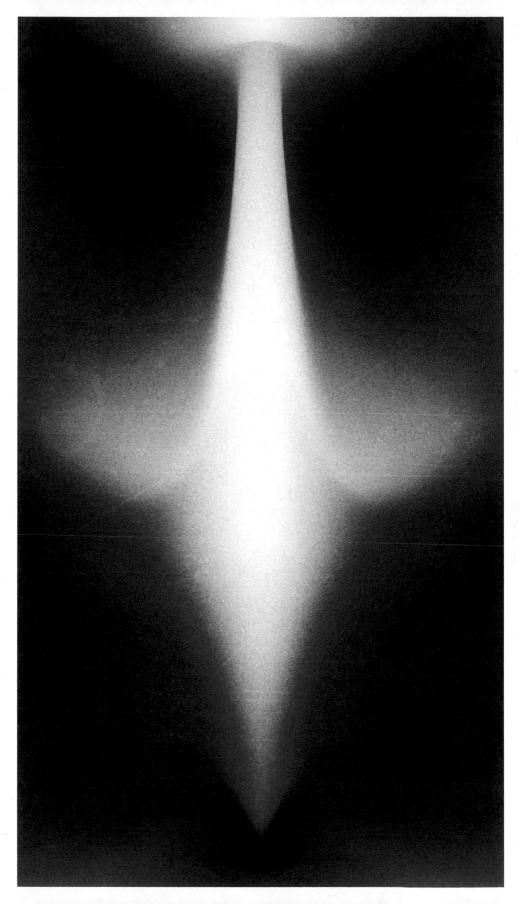

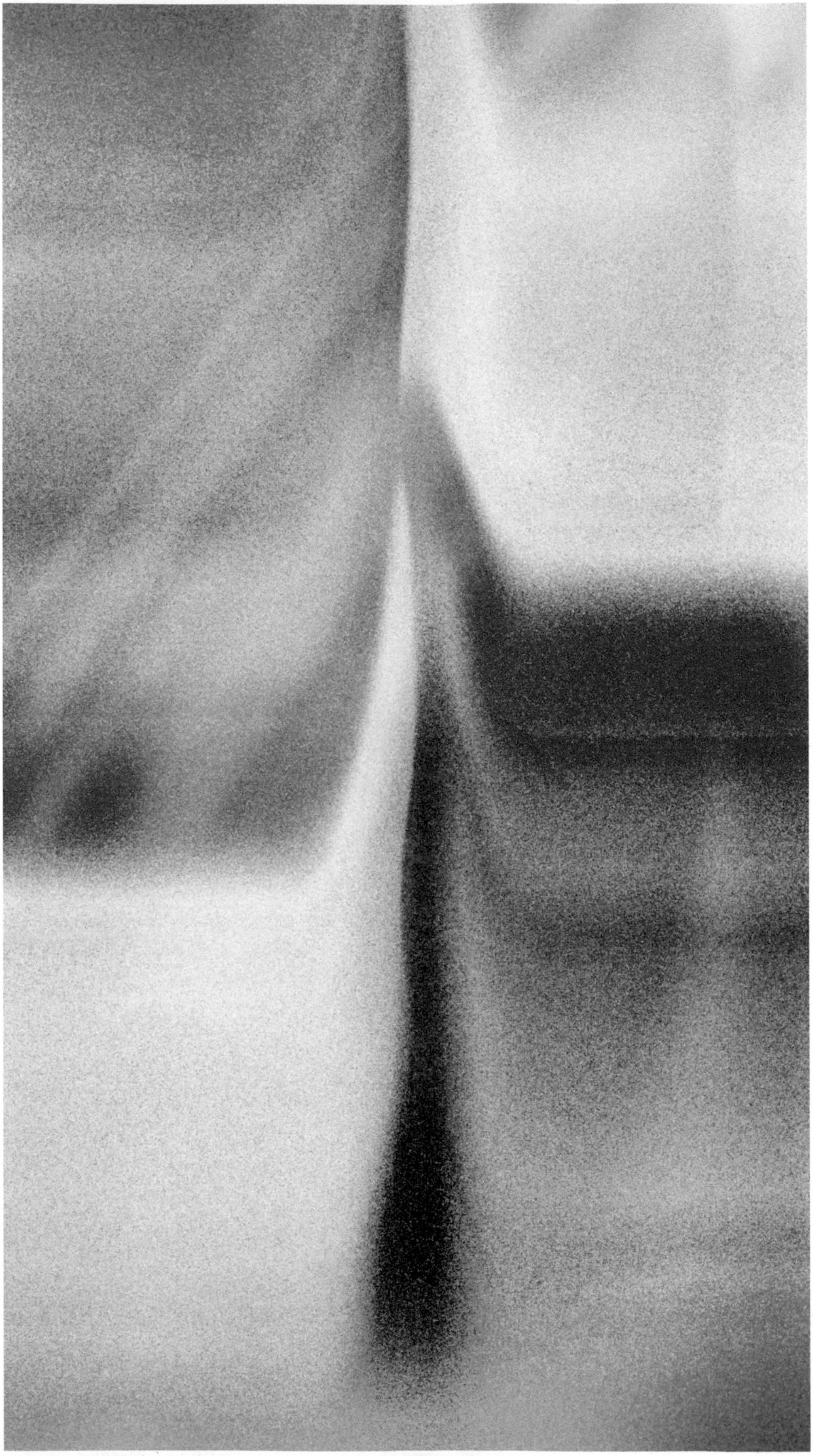

relationship with her mother and a forgotten memory appeared in her mind. Her body contracted and she began to cry. When she was about seven years old, she asked her mother to give her a rabbit that she had seen at a market stall; she wanted to love it and take care of it, she said. She was going to call it Pepe. After a few days, his mother brought it home and told her: "I am giving it to you on the condition that you take care of it, now you're its mother, don't let it die." A few days later, when she got home from school, she found the cage empty. She couldn't remember where she had been negli-

Reality exists as something objective and subjective, as something measurable and as something immeasurable.

gent, but Pepe had disappeared. She was overcome with fear and guilt, and she remembered exactly her mother's words: "You're not capable of taking care of anyone, you're a bad mother! You've killed Pepe!" Those words burned into her mind and her entire body. Her whole body believed that anyone under her care would suffer some misfortune.

After processing that fear and the belief that she was a bad mother, she became pregnant after two months. This therapy wasn't aimed at getting her pregnant through the power of the mind, but that's what happened. To this day I don't know what it was that unlocked her fears and beliefs, if it was induction, placebo, magical thinking, listening to herself or neuroscience. I don't know if it was quantum mysticism or self-deception; I only know that, in some way, the mystical tradition enters into dialogue with the neurosciences: mind and body, right and left, science and spirituality united not to conquer, but to learn. There is, in that *corpus callosum*, a link capable of helping us live in our totality.

Reality exists as something objective and subjective, as something measurable and as something immeasurable. Faith in a God requires the same faith as logic. And, in that process of knowing, the goal should not be the possession of knowledge, salvation or security. It shouldn't be faith from a place of pride, or fear of the different thought systems to our own, or even certainty itself. The goal should be something that is part of the process of human reasoning: the process of acquiring knowledge itself. Not faith, not science, not quantum mysticism. ▲

Adriana Royo is a therapist and psychological advisor specialising in pathologies related to new technologies. She is the author of two books: 'Falos y falacias' (Arpa, 2018) and 'Ética del despiadado' (Ediciones B, 2020).

Marina Colell (@graphitons) works at the intersection between art, quantum physics and technology, developing installations and digital art. In this series she interprets scientific theories and complex ideas with suggestive images.

NO GOD, ONLY RELI- GION

Texto **Samuel Valiente**   ▲   Cover image **Cruz Serna**

Modern life seems to have turned its back on traditional faiths. In Silicon Valley, technological mecca and cultural beacon for the future, religions —and specifically Christianity— have become little less than taboo. But is being a believer really incompatible with a hyperdigital world? What if we're missing something?

With most of the articles in the magazine almost finished, it suddenly dawned on me that in an issue focused on faith, none of the articles are about traditional religions. At first I justified this by considering that, as a publication focused on progress and the future, it didn't make much sense to look back and waste column inches on those archaic, boring and conservative credos. Some time later, with the idea still ringing around in my head, I was more honest with myself: the real reason I didn't want to discuss the issue was, on the one hand, laziness in the face of my own ignorance, and on the other, fear of writing about something that tends to cause tension and rejection, especially among young progressives (who are, as it happens, the majority of our readers). I also realised that I was actually very curious to know the opinion of more or less fervent believers about the questions we typically discuss here. So I decided to ask religious people linked in some way to technology. And yes, it wasn't easy to find them and, in many cases, to convince them to talk to us.

Note: although the initial intention was to speak with believers of different religions, we ended up focusing on Christianity due to proximity to the sources. We have attempted, in any case, to speak more about the experience of faith more broadly than about the details of each particular religion.

THE PROCESSION IS INTERIOR

In one of the most famous scenes of the *Silicon Valley* (HBO) series, protagonist and Pied Piper CEO Richard Hendricks introduces his latest member, the founder of a gay dating app, to the board. The character, in addition to being homosexual, turns out to be Christian. In one of his usual clumsy displays, Richard reveals both facts to the team and unleashes chaos. "You got me out of the closet!" The newcomer complains, only referring to his religion, not his sexual orientation. A few minutes later, his colleagues put their hands to their heads and put Richard into context: "In Silicon Valley, if you're polyamorous, they call you brave. Microdose LSD on your cereal and you're a trailblazer. But the one thing you can't be is Christian."

This gag, which plays with the classic humorous device of role reversal, is hyperbolic for most view-

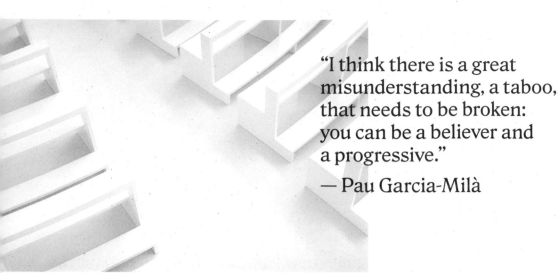

"I think there is a great misunderstanding, a taboo, that needs to be broken: you can be a believer and a progressive."
— Pau Garcia-Milà

ers, but, as I have discovered while writing this article, it's not too far from the religious reality in the world's most advanced valley.

The first believer I come into contact with works between Barcelona and Palo Alto for one of the tech giants. His initial claim is shocking to me: "I can put you in touch with Christians there, but I'm not allowed to speak publicly about my faith." With that I had an idea how delicate the religious question is in this industry. Luckily, he manages to connect me with the parish priest of the church that he usually visits when he is there. Fr. Brian Dinkel gladly agrees to my request: "I really like the idea of looking at the human side of technology, it's an important issue." Dinkel gives mass in one of the many churches that, despite this supposed bad reputation, exist in Silicon Valley. It's a temple with perpetual adoration, that is to say, with 24-hour spiritual service, and is presided over by a huge 10 meter virgin with an almost futuristic metallic finish. "There is a fairly large number of parishioners and visitors involved in the tech industry. There is a greater number of Christians than people are led to believe. The possible misperception may be due to a fear that people have in professing their faith openly," he says. One of those parishioners, we'll call him

Mike, is keen for me not to reveal his real name. Mike works as a machine learning scientist for a tech company and confesses to keeping his faith under wraps: "Many Silicon Valley professionals consider religion to be bigoted and backwards, so Christians, and people of other religions, don't feel comfortable sharing this about themselves," he confesses. Another individual I contact is well-known in Spain, Pau Garcia-Milà, who during the years of the internet boom became the visible face of innovation and young entrepreneurship thanks to his projects and awards. "I'm willing to come out of the closet," he tells me, and immediately I think of that scene in *Silicon Valley*. Pau has never manifested his faith in public (in fact, he's a more or less recent convert), but for some reason he thinks it's about time. "I think there is a great misunderstanding, a taboo, that needs to be broken: you can be a believer and a progressive, although many sectors of the Church don't really like that," he says. His point of view is much more optimistic than Mike's: "I don't think there is discrimination, which is more visible in other groups. They don't kill us for being Christians, at worst you might be considered a retrograde, because there are still many prejudices." Although he also considers that the Church should engage in self-criticism in light of this situation: "we were used to people not asking questions, not being able to doubt, being scolded every Sunday... the good thing is that now you can be a Christian by choice, nobody forces you to be Christian." For him, there is also a total compatibility between hypertechnological life and faith, something that not all believers, as we will see, perceive in the same way.

THE MONTSE MEDINA CASE

OK, I admit it: this article should have been an interview. But the interviewee, who probably could have thrown more light on the matter, or a brighter light (perhaps too bright), didn't answer my call. And that's because she is cloistered in a convent. Yes, she is a contemplative nun, but she hasn't always been one. In fact, she was admitted just a few months ago. Before that, she had achieved it all in the world of tech and business: she had two Master's degrees and a Ph.D. in Computational Mathematical Engineering from Stanford University, founded a start-up in Silicon Valley that was eventually part of the Fortune 100, sold it to PayPal for a huge amount of money and, at just 34 years old, she became a Deloitte partner. But one day she decided to drop everything. And she communicated it through an intense and extensive farewell letter published, of course, on LinkedIn. "I have decided, without any regrets, to stop investing in my earthly future and start investing in my future for eternal life. [...] I am not leaving the world as it were, just the mundane. And I want to give my life in prayer and offering to all those whom God loves," she affirms, with a confidence and poise that is surprising at least in the face of such resignation: nothing less than a great fortune, admirable prestige and the professional effort of an entire life. What could have led her to make such a radical decision at the peak of her career?

"This is not new. In the Gospel it happened constantly: Jesus calls the apostles and they drop

"The world is perfectible. That's our commission. That's why we work. That's why the work is good."
— Ramon Piqué

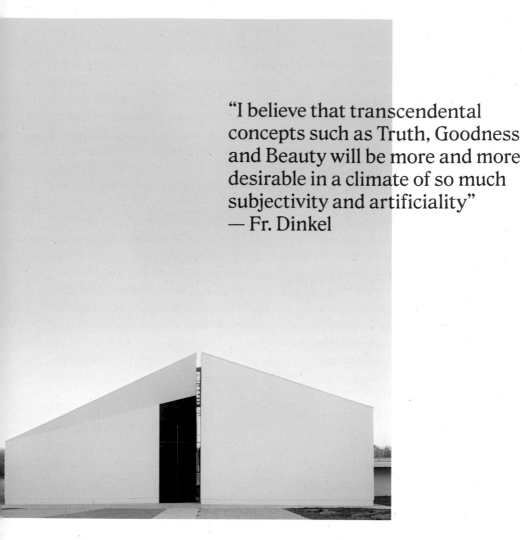

"I believe that transcendental concepts such as Truth, Goodness and Beauty will be more and more desirable in a climate of so much subjectivity and artificiality"
— Fr. Dinkel

everything to follow him," informs Ramon Piqué, creative director and communicator with extensive experience in all kinds of media, digital or otherwise, as well as practicing Christian from an early age. I had had professional contact with him on several occasions and, until they told me about it, I never imagined that he had a deep religious conviction, so I decided to explain Montse's story to him to find out his opinion. "We all know that material wealth is not the important thing in this life. We have experienced it many times, even on a small scale," he explains. "Sometimes these encounters happen, as happened to this girl. Something with such a strong impact that you say: this is what I want, this is what I like, this is what fulfils me and it's true. Or rather: it's *the truth*. And from then on, everything in your life is ordered based on it." He clarifies: "When that happens you don't have to retire to a convent: that was Montse's way, but it doesn't have to be your way." For example, he considers it a mistake to think that one cannot be in the world, the real world, while being religious. "The world is created: by God, by an ordering intelligence, call it the Big Bang if you like, but it is created and designed. And this intelligence adds a second intelligence, humans, to perfect the world. The world is perfectible. That's our commission. That's why we work. That's why the work is good." For him, faith is something internal, although indisputable (he assures that he could not keep it a secret, for example), but above all personal, and involves all aspects of his life, including his work. "It drives me: to be encouraged, to improve, to progress, to do well. Do I see things that are not right? Yes. Do I see people doing things that aren't right? Of course. Do I myself do things that aren't right? Yes. I'm not perfect. But I'm excited about improving every day and contributing to society."

Father Dinkel isn't surprised when I explain Montse's story: "There are cases that actually come from our parish. Three that immediately come to mind are quite similar." According to him, this type of situation will be more and more frequent: "I be-

lieve that transcendental concepts such as Truth, Goodness and Beauty will be more and more desirable in a climate of so much subjectivity and artificiality. This will require us to leave our devices and open our senses to the wonders of creation that surround us, seeking to discover, once again, the goodness and dignity of the human being made in the image and likeness of God".

CRAVING FOR FAITH?

From my point of view that is far removed from any organised religion, and after talking with such devout believers, I cannot help feeling that, somehow, I'm missing something. What if the general feelings of malaise, anxiety, depression and exis-

tential crisis that plague our societies originated precisely from an absence of faith?

Mike explains: "Jesus tells us that to commune with God we must retreat into our 'inner room', meaning the innermost part of our being. The greatest danger of social media and smartphone addiction is the constant stimulation and distraction, which will make us increasingly incapable of interior silence and retreat." A matter that is constantly addressed in this magazine.

Father Dinkel also points to growing artificiality as the cause of our emptiness. "Natural, the objective reality, becomes something foreign to us at best and something to be conquered at worst," he explains, and continues: "There is an excessive emphasis on executing/producing and we have lost the sense of being." On the other hand, he assures that "when God is taken out of the picture, somehow we are left with a horizontal existence (non-transcendental). This means that this world and ourselves become the focal point, the principle of fulfilment. The more that we indulge ourselves in either one of these things —world or self— one realizes that they are good but very limited."

Ramon, for his part, considers that we do yearn for some kind of faith, but that "we are constantly looking for an *à la carte* religion, without sacrifice". "Spiritualized's *No God, Only Religion* comes to mind. We want the spiritual dimension, but without God. We are looking for a supermarket for spiritual goods, an app that helps us meditate. This boom in meditation makes me laugh: I also meditate, but by talking to Jesus!", He says,

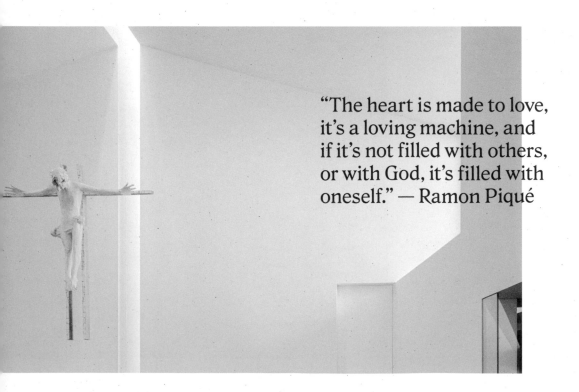

"The heart is made to love, it's a loving machine, and if it's not filled with others, or with God, it's filled with oneself." — Ramon Piqué

giggling. He continues: "People want what fulfils them. And religion is not just about that. If your religion only serves to fill your well-being, your spirituality... it doesn't work. Because we're not made to fill ourselves up like that. The heart is made to love, it's a loving machine, and if it's not filled with others, or with God, it's filled with oneself. And we're not made for that, whether we are Christians or not. The heart cannot be empty."

With these words still echoing in my head, I leave the cafeteria where Ramon and I had met. I light a cigarette. I feel a certain sense of familiarity with everything he has told me, as with what Pau, Mike or Father Dinkel have said, but at the same time I perceive it as distant, as if it were in another language, as if I had missed something important. "I confess that I would like to have faith in something," I tell him, "but I can't make it up." Ramon shrugs and smiles. In the end, I suspect that faith, spirituality, is always on anyone's mind, in some way or another. With greater popular support in some places, lesser support in others. In temples, on tatami mats or in the tranquillity of your bedroom. But as long as we keep asking ourselves questions, it will keep popping up. Ramon sees me off with one last warning: "Faith is an answer, but it's not a pill that erases all your doubts. It doesn't work like that: in fact, it sometimes generates them for you. But, for me at least, that's a reason to live." ▲

1 — Our Lady of Peace Shrine Virgin Mary statue. Santa Clara (Silicon Valley), USA.

2 — St. Bonifatius Kirche. Herbrechtingen, Germany. Kaestle Ocker Architects.

3 & 7 — Hallgrímskirkja Church. Reykjavik, Iceland.

4 & 6 — Chiesa del Buon Ladrone. San Lazzaro di Savena, Italy. IN-OUTarchitettura, LADO architetti, LAMBER + LAMBER

5 — Holy Rosary Complex. Louisiana, USA. Trahan Architects.